Pamela Hammerskog
Eva Wincent

Knitting for Kids

Over 40 Patterns for Sweaters, Dresses,
Hats, Socks, and More for Your Kids

Photography by Rikard Westman

Skyhorse Publishing, Inc.

A thank-you to . . .
Britt Börjesson
Birgitta Esseen
Cecilia af Jochnick
Gunilla Larsson
Gunilla Lindberg
Anna-Lena Lundberg
Herdis Molinder
Mona Westerberg
And also to all of the models and their parents who have shot pictures with us in Tegnérlunden and Vasaparken in Stockholm, at Råsundavägen in Solna, and in Nice, France.

Skyhorse Publishing books may be purchased in bulk at special discounts for sales promotion, corporate gifts, fund-raising, or educational purposes. Special editions can also be created to specifications. For details, contact the Special Sales Department, Skyhorse Publishing, 307 West 36th Street, 11th Floor, New York, NY 10018 or info@ skyhorsepublishing.com.

Skyhorse® and Skyhorse Publishing® are registered trademarks of Skyhorse Publishing, Inc.®, a Delaware corporation.

Photographer: Rikard Westman
Graphic design: Tina Feldreich Danielsson
Layout: Anders Wahlberg

Visit our website at www.skyhorsepublishing.com.

10 9 8 7 6 5 4 3 2 1

Library of Congress Cataloging-in-Publication Data

Hammerskog, Paula.

[Sticka smått. English]

Knitting for kids : over 40 patterns for sweaters, dresses, hats, socks, and more for your kids / Paula Hammerskog and Eva Wincent ; translated from the Swedish by Stine Skarpnes Osttveit.

  pages cm

Includes index.

ISBN 978-1-62087-068-6 (hardcover : alk. paper)

1. Knitting--Patterns. 2. Children's clothing. I. Wincent, Eva. II. Hammerskog, Paula. Sticka smått. Translation of: III. Title.

TT825.H256413 2012

746.43'2--dc23

2012018113

ISBN: 978-1-62087-068-6

Printed in China

Contents

Foreword

In our opinion there are many aspects that distinguish knitting clothes for children from knitting for adults.

The first and most important is that all children's clothes we make are knitted with yarn of very high quality. Nothing can be itchy and it all needs to be machine washable and sturdy; children should not have to worry about taking special care of their knitted clothes.

Many will come to the exact opposite conclusion when it comes to choosing yarn. Since children dirty their clothes or easily get them hooked on things—and also grow out of their clothes so quickly they barely get to use them—people tend to buy cheaper yarn, which is hard and loses its shape after washing. But then we wonder why children refuse to use their knitted clothing . . .

If there is one kind of knitting we should put both money and effort into, it is clothes for children. Soft, strong, and pretty children's clothes are amazingly useful. Furthermore, they can be passed down through generations when made of high-quality yarn and with good care.

One area that often proves challenging when it comes to children's clothes is the sizing. For this book, we have chosen to size according to age, which is the most common way of sizing knitted children's clothes; however, we are well aware that two-year-olds come in many different sizes. Therefore, we have also provided measurements for the clothes so that you can make adjustments based on the specific child.

The gauge is always very important when you knit, but it is especially important here. If you knit even just a tad bit tighter than the given gauge, the garment will end up smaller, and since the clothes are small to begin with this can make a significant difference. When knitting clothes for adults small deviations may not matter as much. That will not work here. You should therefore make a habit of always knitting a small swatch before you begin.

Paula Hammerskog & Eva Wincent

The baby set

Scarf, hat, mittens, and socks knitted in one multicolored yarn are both fun to knit and to wear. The set may also be knitted in a single color for a more classic feel.

SIZES
3–6 (6–9 months)

MATERIALS
Yarn: 2 yarn cones of wool yarn (hosiery yarn striped in colors, which is about 210 m/ 50 g / 1.7 oz.)
Needles: 3 mm / sz 3 and double-pointed needles 3 mm, sz 3

GAUGE
28 st and 38 rows = 4x6 inches / 10x10 cm stockinette on 4 mm / sz 6 needle

Scarf (one size)
Cast on 15 st on 3 mm / sz 3 needle, knit 5 rows.
Continue onto stockinet stitch, except the three outer stitches on each side that you garter stitch. At the same time increase one st on each side on each row until you have 39 stitches total. Knit garter 28 rows.
Decrease 1 st on each row, within the edge stitch, 7 times = 25 stitches.
Knit ribs, k1p1, k1, p1, 1.5 inches / 4 cm, move onto an extra needle, fasten off.
Pick up 25 new stitches over the first rib and knit ribs, k1p1, for 1.5 inches / 4 cm.
Purl these stitches together with the saved stitches so that a tunnel appears.
Increase 12 stitches evenly distributed over the next row = 37 stitches.
Stockinet stitch with 3 edge stitches the same way you did earlier for 10 inches / 25 cm.
Decrease 12 stitches evenly

distributed over the next row.
Knit 1.5 inches / 4 cm of rib knit.
Finish like you did with the first half but decrease within the edge stitch instead of increasing. Bind off.

Mittens (one size)
Cast on 38 stitches, garter knit 3 rows. Continue onto rib knitting and knit k1p1, knit one purl one, until the work measures 2.5 inches / 6 cm.
Increase 1 st on each side and stockinet stitch to 2.5 inches / 6 cm or wanted length.
Decrease: *k6, k2 tog; repeat from * the rest of the row.
Continue to decrease on every other row with one st less between the joining of the stitches until you are left with 10 stitches. Fasten off, pull the tie through the stitch, and fasten. Sew the edge together.
Make a twisted string and thread it through the middle row of the rib knit. Tie a bow. You may also make a longer twisted string that may be fastened on each side.

HAT

Cast on 109 (121) stitches.
Garter knit 5 rows. Continue onto stockinet stitch and start increasing and decreasing the following way:
Knit 1 st, increase 1 st, 17 (19) stockinet stitch, knit 3 stitches together, 18 (20) stitches stockinet stitch, increase 1 st, knit 1 st, increase 1 st, 13 (15) stockinet stitch, knit 3 stitches together, 13 (15) stockinet stitch, increase 1 st, knit 1 st, increase 1 st, 18 (19) stockinet stitch, knit 3 stitches together, 17 (19) stockinet stitch, increase 1 st, knit 1 st.
Continue to increase and decrease on every other row another 11 (13) times, quit on the wrong side.
Next row (garter knit): Knit 18 (20) stitches, 3 stitches together, knit 32 (36) stitches, 3 stitches together, knit 32 (36) stitches, 3 stitches together, knit 18 (20) stitches.
Continue to decrease on every other row until you are left with 25 stitches. Note: There will be 1 st less between the first and last decrease and 2 stitches between the middle decreases.
Conclude with a reverse row, then knit two and two together. Fasten off and pull it through the st.
Sew the hat together and make two twisted ties to tie it together.

SOCKS

Cast on 36 (40) stitches on double-pointed needles; distribute the stitches evenly across four of the needles. Let needles 1 and 4 be the socks' backside and needles 2 and 3 be the front. Rib knit, k1p1, for 24 rows.
Continue with garter stitch until the shaft measures 3.5 (4.5) inches / 9 (11) cm.

THE HEEL

Only knit using needles 1 and 4, save the other stitches for now and do the following:
Garter knit 12 rows in rows back and forth, conclude on the wrong side. Knit 11 stitches, 2 stitches together, knit 1 stitch, turn, purl 4 stitches, 2 purl stitches together, turn, knit 5 stitches, 2 stitches together, knit 1 st, turn. Repeat this process with 1 st more between each turn until all of the heel's stitches are knitted and taken in.

Knit around with all the needles; pick up 10 stitches evenly distributed along the straight edges of the heel, and knit the heel stitches. Continue to knit around, and at the same time decrease 1 st on each side of the needles 1 and 4. (In other words the decrease should be on the backside of the sock, decrease on every other row 7 times.)

THE TOE

Garter knit for 1 (1.2) inch / 2 (3 cm).
Start decreasing for the toe as follows:
Knit 2 stitches together at the end of needles 1 and 3 on the inside of the outer st. In other words, knit until there are 3 stitches left on the needle, knit 2 together, knit 1. On the second and fourth stitch knit 1 slipped st over after the first st, in other words, knit 1, stitch 1 over.
First, decrease on every other row 3 times, followed by increasing on every row 3 times.
Fasten off, pull the tie through the last stitch, and fasten.

The heritage baby set

This baby set was published for the first time by Aktiv hushållning (Active Housekeeping), whose goal is to "give advice and information in response to various housekeeping questions." A knitting enthusiast saved the pattern and since then has knitted the set for her four children, ten grandchildren, and two great-grandchildren. The pattern provided here is an exact copy.

SIZE
Baby

MATERIALS
Yarn: 2x50 m / 50 g / 1.7 oz. of a thin wool yarn (about 210 stitches/ 50g / 1.7 oz.)
Needles: 3 mm / US sz 3 for the cardigan, 2.5 mm / US sz 2 for the hat and double-pointed needles 2 mm / sz 2 for the socks

GAUGE
28 stitches and 36 rows = 4x4 inches / 10x10 cm garter knit on 3 mm / sz 3 needle

CARDIGAN/SWEATER
This sweater, which builds on old pattern descriptions, has been reworked so as to avoid the unpractical tassels and ribbons around the neck, which babies usually want to put in their mouths. It also has few buttons and buttonholes and an emphasis has been made on the sizing of the armhole to ensure that it is easy to put on and take off.

Usually, cardigans are knitted from the bottom up, but in this case you will knit the garment crosswise in one piece. You start with one of the front sides.

Cast on 56 stitches and garter knit 6 rows. Knit the 7th row on the wrong side so that you get a garter-knitted edge where you will fasten the buttons. After which,

continue to garter knit until you have 20 rows altogether. Continue knitting by following this 6-row plan.
Row 1: Knit 44 stitches.
Row 2: Turn and knit 44 stitches back.
Row 3: Knit 50 stitches.
Row 4: Turn and knit 50 stitches back.
Row 5: Knit 56 stitches.
Row 6: Turn and knit 56 stitches back.

By knitting this way you obtain the oscillation around the neckline and at the same time a decorative edge.

Start at row 1 and repeat these 6 rows until you have knitted 61 rows altogether. Then start the arm. Knit from the neck, 23 stitches, cast on 33 new stitches on the same needle, and place the leftover 33 stitches on a safety pin.

Continue the same way as before and turn after 44, 50, and 56 stitches just like the instructions dictate. On the arm you also need to turn at every 6th stitch from the lower edge of the arm every 6th row to ensure that the arm will be positioned correctly. At the bottom a small cuff will appear; if you want this wider, you turn instead at every 10th st from below.

Knit 82 rows, and then bind off the arm's 33 stitches. Take the 33 stitches you placed on the safety pin and the 23 stitches left on the needle and knit the backside by following the 6-row plan until you have 116 rows. Then knit the other arm the same way you knitted the first and then the other front part 61 rows.

Knit 41 rows by following the 6-row plan. After this, garter knit all 56 stitches for 12 rows. The 13th row, which you also garter knit, will be the straight stitch from the neck down; the next row is knitted with purl stitches. In this purled row you will make three button holes the following way: knit 9 stitches, bind off 3 stitches, knit 11 stitches, bind off 3 stitches, knit 11 stitches, bind off 3 stitches, knit 11 stitches, bind off 3 stitches, knit 2 stitches. On the next row,

which you garter knit, you cast on 3 stitches by each button hole to replace the ones you bound off earlier. Then garter knot the last 5 rows and loosely cast off. (If you have trouble doing a nice cast off may use a number 4 needle.)

Pick up 82 stitches at the edge of the neckline and garter knit 1 row. Purl the next row; you are now working on the inside of the cardigan. Continue to knit together 2 and 2 stitches, with the exception of the first 10 and the last 10 stitches, which you knit without knitting the stitches together. Later you garter knit 2 additional rows before you cast off loosely.

If the neck ends up being too tight as the child grows, the neckline can be picked up and re-knitted without knitting as many stitches together.

The arms are now sewn together. Sew a buttonhole seam with split yarn and fasten the buttons in the stockinet-stitched edge.

HAT

A young journalist-mom who once got this hat as a present said that at first she thought it looked very unpractical. But it didn't take long before she was unable to imagine using anything else.

Yarn: 30 g of thin wool yarn.

The first digit is for a baby size, the digit within the parenthesis is for size 6 months, and the third digit is for size 18 months.

The entire hat is garter stitched. Cast on 32 (36) 40 stitches, and knit 1 row. Increase 1 stitch at the end of the first row by picking up the next to last st from the previous row and garter stitch it. Garter stitch the last st as well. The next row is garter stitched until there are only 3 stitches left. Combine two stitches and garter stitch the last. Garter stitch the next row and increase at the end of the row. Continue to increase in one end and decrease in the other, every time you reach the end of the needles.

This small hat is knitted as a zigzag in 6 parts, where the two middle parts contain half the amount of rows as the others.

The first part: Knit 32 (36) 40 rows and do 16 (18) 20 increases and corresponding decreases on each side.

The second part: Knit the same amount of rows as the first part but now increase on the side you decreased earlier and decrease on the side you increased earlier.

The third part: Knit 16 (18) 20 rows and increase and decrease in the opposite ends as the previous part.

The fourth part: Knit 16 (18) 20 rows and increase and decrease in the opposite ends as the previous part.

The fifth part: Knit the same way as part 1.

The sixth part: Knit the same way as part 2, and then bind off.

The hat is now sewn together. The smallest angle should be in the middle of the forehead. Sew it together with the bind off row, and on the backside sew so that the three flaps meet in the middle.

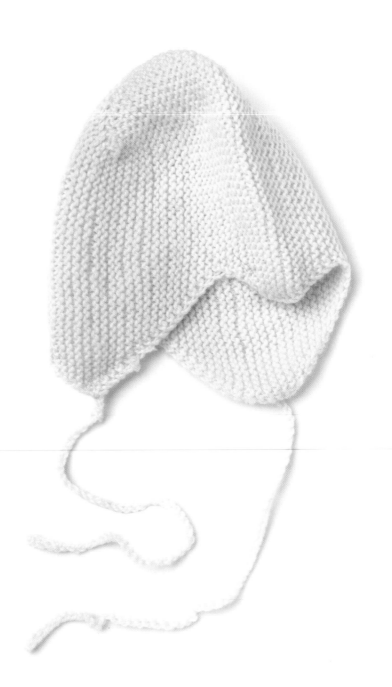

SOCKS

Yarn: 20 g thin wool yarn.

Cast on 48 stitches on each needle. Rib knit in the round (2 garter and 2 purl) for 3.5 inches / 9 cm. Then half the number of stitches by knitting 2 garter stitches together and 2 purl stitches together. Knit 1 cm/ 0.5 inches. Now increase the amount of stitches to the original number. This will create a rib that is good for the calf. Knit the heel with the 1st and 2nd needles. Stockinet stitch for 1.2 inches / 3 cm. Then garter stitch one row with all of the stitches on needle 1.
2nd needle: 1 garter stitch, two stitches together, 1 garter stitch, turn. Purl stitch the needle.
  Next needle: 1 purl stitch, two stitches together, 1 purl stitch, turn. Garter knit the needle.
  Next needle: 2 garter stitch, two stitches together, 1 garter stitch, turn. Knit the rest of the needle.
  Next needle: 2 purl stitch, two stitches together, 1 purl stitch, turn, and so on until all of the stitches have gone. You should be left with 14 stitches.

  Pick up 8 stitches at both sides of the heel. Knit in the round all of the 54 stitches. The ankle stitches should still be ribbed. On every other row decrease one stitch on each end until the stitch number is 48 st. Knit 2.5 inches / 5.5 cm from the heel.

TOE
Garter stitch all stitches and the increase will start on one side first. Knit until 3 stitches are left on the second needle, do a narrowing by knitting two stitches together, garter knit the last stitch. At the beginning of the third needle, garter knit 1 stitch, slip 1 stitch, garter knit 1 stitch, and drag the slipped stitch over the last knitted stitch. Repeat this process on every row. After 7 rows perform this narrowing on the other side as well for 3 rows. The remaining stitches are cast off by knitting 1 stitch from the upper side with 1 stitch from below during casting off.

Sweater with shoulder buttons

The buttons on the shoulder make this sweater easy to put on and take off—a must for baby clothing. The soft and robust yarn makes the garment both easy and quick to knit.

SIZES
3-6 (6-9) 9-12 (12-18) months

MEASUREMENTS
Length: 8.5 (10) 12 (13.5) inches / 22 (26) 30 (34) cm
Periphery: 20.5 (21.5) 23 (23.5) inches / 52 (54) 58 (60) cm
Arm length: 5.5 (6) 7 (9) inches / 14 (16) 18 (22) cm

MATERIALS
Yarn: 4 (5) (7) 8x50 g/ 1.7 oz. of a medium thick cotton yarn (about 85 m/50 g/ 1.7 oz.)
Needles: 3.5 mm / sz 4 and 4 mm / sz 6, two stitch holders, or safety pins
Other: 4 buttons

GAUGE
20 stitches and 28 rows = 4x4 inch / 10x10 cm stockinet stitch on 4 mm / sz 6

BACK PIECE
Cast on 52 (54) 58 (60) stitches on 3.5 mm / sz 4 needle. Stockinet stitch 6 rows. Trade to the 4 mm / sz 6 needle and rib knit, 2 knit, 2 purl, for 4 (4) 6 (6) rows. Continue with stockinet stitches until the work measures 9 (10) 12 (13.5) inches / 22 (26) 30 (34) cm.

SHOULDERS AND NECK
Bind off 15 (15) 16 (16) stitches on each side. Save the middle stitches 22 (24) 26 (28) st on a stitch holder.

FRONT PIECE
Cast on and knit the same way you did for the back piece until the work is 10 (12) 14 (14) rows shorter than the back, counted from the shoulder.

NECK
Knit 23 (23) 24 (24) stitches, turn, and save the other stitches on a spare needle for now. Knit each side separately. Decrease 1 st for the neck on each row 8 times = 15 (15) 16 (16) stitches. Continue without decreasing until the work measures the same as the back piece up by the cast off for the shoulder, finish from the wrong side.

BUTTONHOLE EDGE
Garter knit 1 row.
Buttonhole: 2 garter stitches (1 yarn over, 2 garter stitches together, 3 (3) 3 (3) garter stitches) 2 times, 1 yarn over, 2 garter stitches together, garter stitch the rest of the row.
Garter stitch 1 row. Cast off. Go back to the saved stitches and lift the middle stitches 6 (8) 10 (12) stitches over on a stitch holder. Knit the rest of the row. Decrease 1 stitch for the neck on each row 8 times; continue without decreasing until the work measures the same as the back piece up by the shoulder. Cast off.

ARMS

Cast on 28 (28) 28 (32) stitches on a 3.5 mm / sz 4 mm needle. Garter knit 6 rows. Rib knit 4 (4) 6 (6) rows the same way as before. Change to 4 mm / sz 6 needle and stockinet stitch, at the same time increase 1 st on each side within the 2 outer stitches on every 4th row until you have 48 (52) 56 (58) st. Continue without increasing until the arm measures 5.5 (6.5) 7 (9) inches / 14 (16) 18 (22) cm. Bind off loosely.

COMPLETION

Clamp all of the pieces and place a moist cloth on top and let it dry. You may also press the pieces with a moist towel now and then. Sew the right shoulder together.

NECKBAND

Start by the left shoulder. Pick up 2 stitches from the right side with 3.5 mm / sz 4 mm needle along the buttonhole edge, then 12 (12) 14 (14) stitches along the left front piece. Pick up the saved stitches and garter stitch them. Pick up 12 (12) 14 (14) along the right side, and lastly pick up the saved stitches in the back = 54 (58) 66 (70) stitches. Rib knit two rows, 2 knit, 2 purl. Make a buttonhole on the next row (on the wrong side). Rib knit up until the last 4 stitches, 2 stitches together, slip 1 st, 2 stitches rib knit. Knit 1 additional row rib knit, and then move onto stockinet stitch, which will begin with a row on the wrong side (so that the neckline will roll outwards). Stockinet knit 5 rows more. Loosely cast off.

Place the left shoulder over the right and sew together by the shoulder. Sew the arms and make sure that the middle of the arm meets the middle of the shoulder. Sew side and arm seams. Lightly press on the seams. Sew the buttons on.

Ribbed yoke sweater

What two-year-old does not love running around in a soft and warm yoke sweater? Feel free to knit this sweater a bit large; with the sleeves rolled up it will still fit fine and your child will have something to grow into.

SIZES
3–6 (9–12) 21–18 months

MEASUREMENTS
Length: 10.5 (12) 14 inches /
27 (31) 35 cm
Periphery: 30 (23) 25 inches /
53 (58) 63 cm
Arm length: 6.5 (7) 9 inches /
16 (18) 22 cm

MATERIAL
Yarn: 3 (4) 5 x 50 g/ 1.7 oz. and
1 x 50 g/ 1.7 oz. for the stripes
in a medium thick alpaca
yarn (ca 100 st/50 g/ 1.7 oz.)
Needles: 3.5 mm / sz 4 and
4 mm / sz 6, circular needle
3.5 mm / sz 4 and 4 mm / sz
6, 40 respective 23.5 inch /
60 cm length

GAUGE
22 stitches and 30 rows =
4x4 inch / 10x10 cm stockinet
on 4 mm / sz 6 needle

BACK PIECE
Cast on 57 (63) 67 stitches on 3.5 mm / sz 4 mm needle. Rib knit, 1 knit, 1 purl, for 6 rows. Change to the 4 mm / sz 6 needle and move on to stockinet stitch, at the same time increase one st on the first row. Knit until the work measures 6 (7) 8.5 inches / 15 (18) 21 cm.

RAGLAN ARMHOLES
Cast off 2 stitches on each side. Decrease 1 st on each side on the next row and later on every 4th row 1 (2) 3 times.
Knit 3 rows.
Save the stitches on a stitch holder or an extra needle.

FRONT PIECE
Cast on a needle and knit exactly as instructed for the back piece until you have cast off 2 stitches on each side for the raglan armhole.

NECK
Next row (garter): Knit 1 garter stitch together, then knit until you have 18 (20) 22 stitches on the right needle, turn, and knit each side separately. Cast off 6 stitches at the beginning of the next row, decrease 1 st at the beginning of the next row, cast off 4 (5) 6 stitches at the beginning of the next row. Continue to decrease for the neck on each row 4 times, at the same time decrease for the raglan on every 4th row like before until you are left with 2 stitches. Knit the stitches together and pull the yarn through. Go back to the saved stitches and lift them over the middle stitches 18 (20) 20 st on a stitch holder, then finish knitting the row.
Finish like you did on the first side but mirrored.

ARMS
Cast on 35 (37) 37 stitches on a 31/2 mm needle. Rib knit, 1 knit,

1 purl for 6 rows. Change to the 4 mm / sz 6 needle and stockinet stitch, at the same time increase 1 st on the first row so that you have 36 (38) 38 stitches. Continue to increase 1 st on each side on every 6th row until you have 50 (52) 56 stitches. Continue without increasing until the arm measures 6.5 (7) 4.5 inches / 16 (18) 22 cm.

RAGLAN

Cast off 2 stitches on each side. Decrease 1 stitch on each side on the next row and later on every 4th row 2 (3) 3 times = 40 (40) 44

stitches. Knit 1 row and save the stitches on a stitch holder.

Completion

Clamp all of the pieces, place a moist cloth on top, and let it dry. Sew the raglan seams together.

Yoke

Work on the right side with a circular needle, 4 mm / sz 6. Knit over the saved 40 (40) 44 stitches on the left arm, pick up 18 (19) 22 stitches along the left side of the front neck, knit over the saved 18 (20) 20 stitches mid-front, then

pick up 18 (19) 22 stitches along the right side front, knit over the saved 40 (40) 44 stitches on the back piece = 184 (192) 208 stitches. Knit the yoke in stripes, 4 rows blue and 2 rows white, until you have 3 white stripes, continue with the blue yarn only and knit round like this:

Row 1-5: Rib knit, 4 knit, 4 purl, needle out.

Decrease row 1: 4 knit, 1 purl, 2 purl together, 1 purl, repeat until you finish row. Rib knit 4 rows, 4 knit, 3 purl.

Decrease row 2: 4 knit, 1 2 purl together, 1 purl, repeat until you finish row. Rib knit 4 rows, 4 knit, 2 purl.

Decrease row 3: 1 knit, 2 knit together, 1 knit, 2 purl , repeat out needle.

Rib knit 4 rows, knit 3, purl 2.

Decrease row 4: 1 knit, 2 knit together, 2 purl, repeat out needle. Rib knit 3 rows, knit 2, purl 2.

Decrease row 5: 2 knit, 2 purl together. Repeat out needle. Change to the circular needle 3.5 mm / sz 4 mm and rib knit 8 (10) 10 rows, knit 2, purl 1. Increase 1 st through knitting 2 stitches in the purled stitch. Stockinet stitch 4 rows. Cast off. Sew the sides and arm seams together and press down lightly on the seams.

Striped seaman's sweater

This seaman's sweater is easier to knit than you might think. The only thing that is somewhat challenging is the assembling at the end. If you take care while doing this part you will end up with fantastic results.

SIZE
0–3 (3–6) 6–12 (12–18) months

MEASUREMENTS
Length: 11.5 (13.5) 15.5 (17.5) inches / 23 (27) 31 (35) cm
Periphery: 24.5 (27) 29.5 (31.5) inches / 47 (54) 59 (63) cm
Arm length: 5.5 (6.5) 7 (8.5) inches / 14 (16) 18 (22) cm

MATERIALS
Yarn: a medium thick cotton yarn (ca 115 st/50 g/ 1.7 oz./ 1.7 oz.)

AMOUNTS:
Color A, marine blue: 3 (3) 4 (4) balls
Color B, nature white: 2 (2) 3 (3) balls
Color C, red: 1 ball
Needles: 2.5 / sz 2 and 3.5 mm / sz 4 / sz 4 mm / sz 6

GAUGE
23 stitches and 28 rows = 4x4 inches / 10x10 cm stockinet stitch on 3.5 mm / sz 4 mm / sz 4 needle

BACK PIECE
Cast on 54 (62) 68 (72) stitches with color C on 2.5 mm / sz 2 needle. Rib knit, knit 2, purl 2, for 6 rows. Change to 3.5 mm / sz 4 mm / sz 4 needle and stockinet stitch. Knit stripes the following way:
Row 1–2: Color B.
Row 3–4: Color A.
Row 5–6: Color B.
Row 7–10: Color A.
Repeat row 1-10.
Knit until the work measures 9 (10) 12 (13.5) inches / 22 (26) 30 (34) cm.

NECK AND SHOULDERS
Cast off 7 (8) 8 (9) stitches, knit until you have 10 (11) 12 (12) stitches on the right needle, turn, and knit each side separately. Save the other stitches on the needle for now. Cast off 3 stitches at the beginning of the next row (for the neck).
Cast off the last 7 (8) 8 (9) stitches on each side every other row. Cast off the middle stitches 20 (24) 28 (30) stitches, knit until the row is finished. Complete like you did on the first side but mirrored.

FRONT PIECE
Cast on and knit the same way you did for the back piece until the work is 1.5 (1.5) 2 (2.5) inches / 4 (4) 5 (6) cm shorter than the back when measured from the first cast off on the shoulder.

NECK
Knit 20 (24) 26 (28) stitches, turn, and knit each side separately. Save the other stitches on the needle. Cast off 3 stitches at the beginning of the next row, then decrease 1 st for the neck on every row 3 (5) 6 (7) times. Knit until the front measures the same as the back up by the shoulder (make sure that you are at the same edge as the back). Cast off 7,7 (8,8) 8,9 (9,9) stitches for the shoulder on every other row. Go back to the saved stitches and cast off

the middle stitches 14 (14) 16 (16) for the neck. Complete the same way as you did for the first side but mirrored.

ARMS

Cast on 42 (46) 46 (50) stitches with color C on a 2.5 mm / sz 2 needle. Rib knit, knit 2, purl 2, for 6 (8) 8 (10) rows. Change to a 3.5 mm / sz 4 needle and stockinet and knit stripes the same way as before. Increase 1 st on each side on every 4th row until you have 21.5 (23.5) 26 (14) inches / 54 (60) 66 (72) cm. Cast off.

COMPLETION

Clamp all of the pieces, place a moist cloth on top, and let it dry, or press lightly on the parts with a damp cloth now and then.
Sew the right shoulder together. Pick up 80 (86) 98 (106) stitches of color A from the garter side around the neck. Rib knit, 2 knit, 2 purl, for 4 rows, cast off with garter stitches. Sew the left shoulder together and the short part of the neckline. Sew the arms, and make sure that the middle of the arm is aligned with the middle of the shoulder. Sew side and arm seams together. Press lightly on the seams.

LOOSE SEAMAN'S COLLAR

Cast on 66 stitches with color A on a 2.5 mm/ sz 2 needle. Garter knit 3 rows, change to 3 mm / sz 3 needle, and stockinet. Garter knit the 3 last stitches on each row so that you get a garter stitched edge. Knit until the work measures 4 inches / 10 cm.
Cast off the middle 25 stitches and knit each side separately. Keep the other stitches on a spare needle. Every 3rd row, decrease 1 st on the inside of the 3 edge stitches on the collar. At the same time increase 1 st on the inside every 4th row.

Continue to decrease and increase until you are left with three stitches. Cast off.
Go back to the saved stitches and knit the other side the same way, except in the opposite direction.

Decorative Ribbon: Cast on 5 stitches of color B on 2.5 mm / sz 2 needle, garter knit until the ribbon measures 3 inches / 8 cm. Cast off. Sew the short ends together and thread in through the collar flaps; sew them on with a few stitches on the front piece. Sew the collar on along the neckline in the back.

Short-sleeved tunic

A sweet tunic in a lace pattern is accompanied here by a pair of shorts in a matching color (see p. 40). Soft and classic baby colors makes for a clean look.

SIZES
0–3 (3–6) 6–9 (9–12) 12–18 months

MEASUREMENTS
Length: 10 (10.5) 11.4 (12) 13 inches / 25 (27) 29 (31) 33 cm
Periphery: 20 (20) 20.5 (21.5) 22 inches / 48 (50) 52 (54) 56 cm
Arm length: 1.5 (1.5) 2 (2.5) 3 inches / 4 (4) 5 (6) 7 cm

MATERIALS
Yarn: 3 (4) 4 (5) 5 balls of a thin cotton yarn (about 140 m/50 g/ 1.7 oz.)
Needles: 1.2 mm / sz 2.5 and 3 mm / sz 3
Other: 1 small button if needed

GAUGE
28 stitches and 38 rows = 4x4 inch / 10x10 cm stockinet stitch on 3 mm / sz 3 needle

BACK PIECE
Cast on 95 (103) 111 (119) 127 stitches on 2 1.2 mm / sz 2.5 needles. Garter knit 6 rows. Change to 3 mm / sz 3 needle and knit lace pattern, repeat the 16 pattern rows until the work measures 7 (7.5) 8.5 (9) 9 inches / 18 (19) 21 (22) 23 cm, complete on the wrong side. Stockinet stitch 2 rows, increase with 1 st at the end of the last row.
Decrease the following way: garter knit 4 (6) 8 (10) stitches, knit the stitches together two at a time until you are left with 4 (6) 8 (10) 12 stitches, garter knit the rest of the needle. Continue with stockinet stitch, knit 4 rows.

ARMHOLES
Cast off 4 (4) 6 (6) 6 stitches on each side. Knit until the armhole measures 2.5 (3.5) 4 (4.5) 5 inches / 7 (9) 10 (11) 12 cm.

NECK
Cast off the middle 22 (22) 22 (24) 24 stitches and knit each side separately. Keep the other stitches on a needle. Decrease 1 stitch for the neck on each row 3 times. Knit 1 cm / 0.5 inch, cast off the last 8 (11) 12 (14) 17 stitches. Repeat on the other side in the opposite direction.

FRONT PIECE
Cast on and knit like the back piece until the work is 1.5 (2) 2.5 (3) 3 inches / 4 (5) 6 (7) 8 cm shorter than the back, measured from the shoulder.

NECK
Cast off the middle 16 (18) 18 (20) 20 st for the neck and knit each side separately. Keep the other st on a needle. Decrease 1 st for the neck on each row, 4 times, then on every other row until you are left with 8 (11) 12 (14) 17 st. Continue until the front measures the same

TIPS & TRICKS

■ The tunic is very pretty when knitted in black as well. Black is an unusual color on babies, but the result is very cool.
■ If the tunic is knitted in stockinet stitch it will also get a tougher look.
■ There is also a hat that goes with this tunic; see photo on p. 47 and pattern on p. 49.

PATTERN DIAGRAM

Read the diagram from the right to the left.

Empty box=stockinet
o = yarn over
\= slip 1 stitch, knit 1 stitch, pass slip stitch over (sl1, k1, psso)
/= purl 2 together

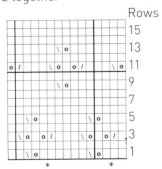

Start here
Repeat row 1–16 and the 8 patterns in between * and *

as the back up by the shoulder. Cast off. Knit the other side the same way, but mirrored.

ARMS

Cast on 44 (52) 62 (68) 74 st on 2.5 mm / sz 2 needle and garter knit 6 rows. Increase to 47 (55) 63 (71) 79 st evenly distributed across the last row. Change to 3 mm / sz 3 needle and knit pattern, increase 1 stitch on each side, every 4th row until you have 51 (61) 69 (75) 81 stitches, knit the new stitches with stockinet stitch. Cast off when the arm measures 2.5 (2.5) 2.5 (3) 3 inches / 6 (6) 6 (7) 8 cm.

COMPLETION

Press the pieces lightly on their backside with a damp cloth.
Sew the shoulder together. Pick up 77 (79) 81 (85) 87 st evenly distributed from the garter side on a 2.5 mm / sz 2 needle. Garter knit 4 rows, loosely cast off with garter stitches.
Check the neckline and make sure that the width is correct; you may need a button by the shoulder. In that case, sew half of the other shoulder together (leave it open by the neck). Sew a buttonhole on the neckline and sew a button on the other side. Sew the arms together, and keep the last straight part of the arm aligned with the cast off stitches in the armhole. Sew side seams and arm seams. Lightly press on the seams.

Shorts

The shorts are knitted in a single piece and are therefore quick to knit and stitch. Shorts can be paired with tunics to provide a nice outfit. The description of the tunic is on p. 22.

SIZES
0–3 (3–6) 6–9 months

MEASUREMENTS
Length: 9 (10) 11.5 inches / 22 (26) 30 cm
Waist: 15 (18.1) 20.5 inches / 38 (46) 52 cm

MATERIALS
Yarn: 2 (2) 2 x 50 g/ 1.7 oz. of a thin yarn in a wool/cashmere/microfiber mixture (ca 140 m/50g)
Needles: 2.5 sz 2 and 3 mm / sz 3.
Other: elastic band

GAUGE
28 st and 36 rows = 4x4 inch / 10x10 cm stockinet stitch on 3 mm / sz 3 needle

SHORTS
(Knitted all in one piece)
Cast on 62 (70) 72 stitches on 2.5 mm / sz 2 needle. Rib knit, knit 1, purl 1, for 10 rows.
Change to 3 mm / sz 3 needle. Continue with stockinet stitch and increase 1 st on each side on the 5th row, continue to increase on every 6th row until you have 78 (86) 94 stitches. Knit for an additional 5 rows.

LEGS
Cast off 3 stitches at the beginning of each row until you have 12 (20) 22 st. Knit back mirrored, in other words cast on 3 st at the end of every row (see knit cast on p.112) until you have 78 (86) 94 stitches once more. Knit an additional 5 rows (end from the wrong side). Decrease 1 st on each side at the 5th row and later on every 6th row until you are left with 62 (70) 72 st. Knit 7 rows.

Shape the top-part of the pant the following way:

Row 1: Garter knit up until the last 7 (8) 9 st and turn.

Row 2: Purl stitch up until the last 7 (8) 9 st and turn.

Row 3: Garter knit up until the last 14 (16) 18 st and turn.

Row 4: Purl stitch up until the last 14 (16) 18 st and turn.

Row 5: Garter stitch up until the last 21 (24)27 st and turn.

Row 6: Purl stitch up until the last 21 (24) 24 st and turn.

Row 7: Garter stitch up until the last 28 (32) 36 st and turn.

Row 8: Purl stitch all stitches. Change to 2.5 mm / sz 2 needle and rib knit, knit 1, purl 1 for 10 rows.

Cast off in a rib knit.

RIBBED AROUND THE LEGS

Pick up 68 (70) 72 st around the legs and rib knit, knit 1, purl 1, for 6 (8) 10 rows.

COMPLETION

Clamp all of the pieces like the shorts and place a damp cloth on top; let it dry. Sew the sides together and lightly press the seams. Sew the elastic band in the waist together.

Tunic with ruffled edges

A thick sweater with ruffled edges at the waist and wrists is delightful for a baby to wear when the stroller feels a little cold or in the embrace of mom or dad. Wool is a wonderful material for children, blended here with some cotton for a softer feel.

SIZES
3–6 (6–12) 12–18 months

MEASUREMENTS
Length: 10 (12) 13.5 inches / 26 (30) 34 cm
Periphery: 22 (23.5) 25 inches / 56 (60) 64 cm
Arm length: 6 (7) 8 inches / 16 (18) 20 cm

MATERIALS
Yarn: 4 (5) 6 x 50 g/ 1.7 oz. of a medium-thick wool and cotton yarn (about 115 st/50g)
Needles: 4 mm / sz 6 and double-pointed needles or a short circular needle 3 mm / sz 3
Other: 1 button

GAUGE
22 stitches and 30 rows = 4x4 inch / 10x10 cm stockinet stitch on 4 mm / sz 6 needle

BACK PIECE
Start with the ruffles and cast on 288 (304) 320 st on the 4 mm / sz 6 needle.
Row 1: Knit 2, lift the 1st stitch over the other, repeat for the rest of the row. (The number of stitches should now be half of what you started with.)
Row 2: Purl 2 together, repeat for the rest of the row.
(Now you've reached the final number of stitches.)
Knit stockinet stitch for 2 rows. Start decreasing in the ends the following way:
Knit 3, knit 2 together, knit up until the last 5 st, slip 1 stitch, knit 1 stitch, pass slip stitch over, knit 3.
Repeat the decrease on every 8th row until you are left with 62 (66) 70 stitches. Continue without decreasing until the work measures 6 (8) 8.5 inches / 16 (20) 21 cm.

ARMHOLE
Cast off 3 st in each side = 56 (60) 64 st. Continue to decrease 1 st on each side on every other row 3 times. Decrease on the inside of the 3 outer st the same way as before = 50 (54) 58 st. Continue without decreasing until the armhole measures 3 (3) 3.5 inches / 7 (8) 9 cm, finish on the wrong side.

SPLIT
Knit 25 (27) 29 st, turn and save the other stitches on a needle for now. Knit each side separately.
Next row (wrong side): Knit 2, knit the rest of the row on the wrong side.
New row (straight):
Garter knit 2 stitches closest to the split and the rest of the stitches with stockinet stitch. Continue until the armhole measures 4.5 (5) 5 inches / 11 (12) 13 cm, finish on the wrong side.

SHOULDER
Cast off 12 (13) 14 st for the shoulder, knit the row all the way through. Cast off the remaining 13 (14) 15 st. Go back to the saved stitches, and finish like you did on the first side but mirrored.

FRONT PIECE

Cast on and knit like you did with the back piece, until the armhole measures 3 (3.5) 4 inches / 8 (9) 10 cm.

NECK

Cast off the middle 14 (16) 18 st for the neck and knit each side separately. Save the other stitches on a needle for now. Cast off 3 st for the neck. Decrease 1 st for the neck on each row until you are left with 12 (13) 14 st.
Continue without decreasing until the front piece measures the same as the back. Cast off.
Go back to the saved stitches and finish like the first but mirrored.

ARMS

Cast on 160 (168) 176 st on a 4 mm / sz 6 needle. Do a ruffle edge the same way as before = 40 (42) 44 st. Knit stockinet stitch and increase 1 st on each side, on the inside of the 3 outer st, on every 4th row until you have 56 (58) 62 st. Continue without increasing until the arm measures 8 (9) 10 inches / 16 (18) 20 cm.

SLEEVE CAP

Cast off 3 st on each side. Decrease the same way as before and de-crease 1 st on each side every other row, 4 times, keep on the inside of the outer 3 stitches = 42 (44) 46 st. Knit 1 row, cast off.

COMPLETION

Clamp all of the pieces and place a damp cloth on top; let it dry.
Sew both shoulders together.

NECKLINE

Start and end by the split, pick 68 (74) 80 st evenly distributed around the neck from the right side with the double-pointed needles. Garter knit 2 rows, cast off with scalloped edge the following way:
Cast off 1 st straight, lift the stitch back on the left needle, cast on 2 new stitches (by knitting 1 st and casting on the left stick, repeat once more = 2 cast on st). Cast off 3 st, repeat the rest of the row. Make a buttonhole up by the neck; sew a button on the other side. Sew the side and arm seams together. Sew the arms. Gently press the seams.

Patterned baby cardigan and socks

This is a real classic. The pattern for this lovely cardigan and socks comes from the book Vi syr, vi sticker, vi virkar (We Sew, We Knit, We Serve) from the 1940s. We love it as the cardigan is both fun to knit and pretty.

SIZES
0–3 (3–6) 9–12 months

MEASUREMENTS CARDIGAN
Periphery: 18 (21)23 inches / 46 (54) 59 cm
Length: 8.5 (9.5) 11 inches / 21 (24) 28 cm

MEASUREMENTS SOCKS
Length: 3.5 inches / 9 cm

MATERIALS
Yarn: 2 (3) 4 x 50 g/ 1.7 oz. + 1 ball for the hat and socks of a thin wool or cotton yarn (about 160 m/50 g/ 1.7 oz.)
Needles: 2 and 3 mm / sz 3, one stitch holder
Other: 3 buttons, elastic band for the socks

GAUGE
25 st and 60 rows = 4x4 inch / 10x10 cm pattern stitch on 3 mm / sz 3 needle

CARDIGAN
BACK AND FRONT PIECE
(Both are knitted in one piece up until the armhole.)
Cast on 148 (156) 164 st on 3 mm / sz 3 needle. Garter knit 3 rows, continue with the pattern, and do the following:
Row 1 and all odd rows: Garter knit.
Row 2: Garter knit 7 st, * purl 2, knit 2; repeat from * until the last 9 st that you knit purl 2, knit 7.
Row 4: As row 2.
Row 6: Garter knit 7 st * knit 2, purl 2, repeat from * until the last 9 st that you garter stitch.
Row 8: Like row 6.
Repeat rows 1–8 and knit the outer 7 st on each side in garter stitch (front edges). Continue the pattern until the work measures 5 (5.5) 6.5 inches / 13 (14) 16 cm. Then cast off for the armholes the following way:
Knit 38 (40) 42 st, cast off 5 st, Knit 62 (66) 70 st, cast off 5 st,

Knit the rest of the row.
First knit the left front piece:
Continue with pattern and front edge as earlier, decrease 1 st for the armhole on every other row, 8 (9) 10 times = 30 (31) 32 st. Cut the yarn and save the st on a stitch holder, knit the back piece and decrease for the armhole the same way = 46 (48) 50 st. Cut the yarn and save the stitches on a stitch holder. Knit the right front piece just like the left but mirrored.
Leave the work for now.

ARMS
Cast on 34 (38) 42 st on 3 mm / sz 3 needle, garter knit 14 rows, increase 8 st evenly distributed over the last row. Continue with the pattern; in addition, increase 1 st on each side on every 6th row 5 times = 52 (56) 60 st. Continue without increasing until the arm measures 5 (6.5) 7.5 inches / 13 (16) 19 cm.

Cast off 3 st on each side for the armhole, then decrease 1 st on each side on every other row 8 (9) 10 times = 30 (32) 34 st. Save the stitches on a needle.

KNIT THE CARDIGAN TOGETHER

First knit the right front piece up until the last st, which you knit together with the first stitch on the one arm. Knit the arm up until the last st, which is knitted with the first st on the back piece. Knit the back piece up until the last st, which is knitted together with the first st on the next arm. Knit the arm to the last st, which is knitted together with the first stitch on the left front piece = 162 (170) 178 st. Continue to garter knit the front edges. Rib knit the rest of the stitches, knit 1, purl 1 (decrease 1 st as well so that the number of stitches become uneven), rib knit 1.5 (2) 2.5 inches / 4 (5) 6 cm. At the same time make buttonholes on the left front piece (this is boy-buttoning, if you are knitting for a girl the buttonholes should be made on the right front piece). Make the first buttonhole on the 3rd rib knit row, the other on the 9th (11th) 13th. (The third buttonhole will end up by the neckline.) Knit the buttonholes on the front edge together the following way:

knit 2, knit 2 together, 1 yarn over, knit 3.
Continue with the front edges like before. Knit the rib knit stitches together two and two until you finish the row.
Change to 2 mm needle, garter knit, and decrease 8 st evenly distributed over the first row. Garter knit 14 rows and make the last buttonhole on the 5th row. Cast off.

COMPLETION
Clamp all of the pieces. Place a damp cloth on top and let it dry. Sew the arms together. Sew the armholes together. Sew on the buttons.

GARTER KNITTED SOCKS
(one size)
Cast on 40 st on a 3 mm needle and rib knit 3 inches / 7 cm, knit 1, purl 1. Move 13 st on the right side and 14 st on the left side onto two safety pins. Garter knit 15 rows over the middle 13 st (this creates the upper side), save the st for now. Knit over all st, at the same time pick up 10 st along the short sides of the upper side = 60 st. Garter knit 2 st with all stitches. Continue to knit with the middle 12 st, let the 24 stitches on each side

rest for now, at the same time knit the last stitch together with the first stitch of the resting stitches until you are left with 7 stitches on each side, knit the row finished = 26 st. Cast off the following way: cast off 5 st * knit the next 2 st together, cast off *, repeat *-* once, cast off 8 st, repeat *-* 2 times, cast off the last 5 stitches. Sew all of the seams together, and turn the seam outwards and up since the shaft is now folding outwards. Sew the elastic band on the middle of the rib cuff and on the inside.

Classic cardigan with raglan sleeve

This classic cardigan is so well-loved that it has been tagging along for years. It is knitted for a two-year-old, but my now four-year-old Beatrice refuses to let it go. The three-quarter sleeve and tight waist are just as modern as the traditional shape.

SIZES
3–6 (6–9) 12–24 months

MEASUREMENTS
Length: 10 (11.5) 12.5 inches / 25 (29) 32 cm
Periphery: 20 (22) 23.5 inches / 50 (55) 60 cm
Arm length 6.5 (7) 9 inches / 16 (18) 22 cm

MATERIALS
Yarn: 4 (5) 5x50 g/ 1.7 oz. of a medium thick wool yarn (about 125 m/50 g/ 1.7 oz.)
Needles: 3 mm/ sz 3 and 4 mm / sz 6
Other: 6 buttons

GAUGE
22 st and 30 rows = 4x4 inch / 10x10 cm stockinet stitch on 4 mm / sz 6 needle

BACK PIECE
Cast on 57 (63) 69 st on a 3 mm / sz 3 needle, garter knit 6 rows. Change to 4 mm / sz 6 needle and stockinet stitch, knit until the work measures 6 (7) 8 inches / 15 (17) 20 cm.

RAGLAN
Cast off 2 st on each side. Perform the decreasing on the right side the following way: garter knit 2, garter knit 2 together, garter knit the rest of the row. Decrease on every other row until you are left with 13 (15) 17 stitches; complete the work on the right side.

LEFT FRONT PIECE
Cast on 34 (36) 40 st on 3 mm / sz 3 needle, garter knit 5 rows. Garter knit 5 stitches, lift the 5 stitches over on a safety pin (this will be the front edge later) and finish the row with a garter stitch. Change to 4 mm / sz 6 needle and stockinet stitch, knit until the work measures the same as the back by the cast off for raglan.

RAGLAN
Cast off 2 stitches in the beginning of each row. Do the decreases on the right side the following way: garter knit 2, garter knit 2 together, garter knit the rest of the row. Decrease on every other row until you are left with 13 (15) 17 st; finish on the right side of the work.

NECK
Cast off 3 st at the beginning of every row. Continue decreasing for raglan the same way as before. Knit 2 st together for the neck on each row until you are left with 2 stitches. Knit the last 2 stitches together and thread the yarn though the st.

RIGHT FRONT PIECE
Cast on 34 (36) 40 st, garter knit 4 rows. Make a buttonhole on the next row: knit 1, knit 2 together, 1 yarn over, garter knit the rest of the row. Next row: knit up until the last 5 stitches, turn and move the last 5 stitches onto a safety pin; finish knitting the row on the wrong side.

Change to 4 mm / sz 6 needle, and knit the right front piece like the left piece but mirrored.

ARMS

Cast on 36 (36) 38 st on a 3 mm / sz 3 needle, garter knit 6 rows. Switch to 4 mm / sz 6 needle and stockinet stitch. Increase 1 st on each side on every 4th row until there are 54 st, later on every 6ths row until you have 56 (60) 62 st. Continue without increasing until the arm measures 6.5 (7) 9 inches / 16 (18) 22 cm.

RAGLAN

Cast off 2 st on each side. Do the decreases for the raglan the same way you did for the back piece until you have 20 st left.

LEFT ARM

Decrease 1 st on each side, knit 1 row, cast off 4 st at the beginning of the next row (for the neck).

Decrease 1 st at the beginning of the next row, cast off 6 st at the beginning of the next row, knit the rest of the needle. Cast off.

RIGHT ARM

Cast off 5 st at the beginning and decrease 1 st at the end of the next row.
Knit 1 row.
Cast off 5 stitches in the beginning and decrease 1 st at the end of the next row.
Knit 1 row. Cast off.

COMPLETION

Clamp all of the pieces. Sew the raglan seams together.

BUTTONHOLE EDGE

Knit the same way as the first edge, make buttonholes corresponding to the markings for buttons the same way you made the first buttonhole. Fasten the front edges by sewing them along the front pieces.

COLLAR

Start and end at the middle of the garter knitted front edges. Pick up 73 (77) 83 st with a 3 mm / sz 3 needle evenly distributed around the neck. Garter knit until the collar measures 2 (2.5) 3 inches / 5 (6) 7 cm. Loosely cast off.
Gently press the seams with a damp cloth. Sew the buttons on.

TIPS & TRICKS

■ Make buttonholes on the left front if you want it buttoned for a boy.
■ It is easy to make the cardigan without a collar. Do not bind off the edge, but save it on a safety pin. Make 5 buttonhole edges and score the last buttonhole on the edge of the neck. Pick up the saved st on a sz 3 needle, pick up around 69 (73) 79 st around the neck, knit 2 rows. Make the last buttonhole above the other, knit 3 more rows, and bind off.

Wrap-around cardigan

The vivid color makes this rather attractive sweater a lot edgier than it would be in milder shades. Soft blue, green, pink, and beige colors would create a completely different garment.

SIZES
0–6 (6–12) 12–24 months

MEASUREMENTS
Length: 10 (14.5) 15.5 inches / 25 (29) 33 cm
Periphery: 12 (25.5) 29 inches / 44 (51) 58 cm
Arm length: 7 (8) 9 inches / 14 (16) 18 cm

MATERIALS
Yarn: 2 (3) 4 x 50g of a thin wool yarn (about 160 m/50 g/ 1.7 oz.)
Needles: 2.5 and 3 mm / sz 3, 2.5 mm / sz 2 circular needle, 40 inches / 80 cm long

GAUGE
28 st and 36 rows = 4x4 inch / 10x10 cm stockinet stitch on 3 mm / sz 3 needle

BACK PIECE
Cast on 61 (71) 81 st on 2.5 needle, garter knit 3 rows. Switch to 3 mm / sz 3 needle and start knitting pattern after the diagram (see p. 37), repeat the 8 pattern rows 3 times, continue with stockinet stitch until the work measures 5 (6) 7 inches / 12 (15) 18 cm.

ARM HOLES
Cast off 4 st on each side. Continue with stockinet stitch until the armhole measures 5 (5) 5.5 inches / 12 (13) 14 cm.

SHOULDERS
Cast off the middle 11 (13) 15 st for the neck; knit each side separately. Cast off 3 st against the neck at the beginning of the next row, finish knitting the row. Cast off the remaining 18 (22) 26 stitches for the shoulder. Do the other side the same way but mirrored.

LEFT FRONT PIECE
Cast on 54 (64) 74 st on 2.5 mm needle, garter knit 3 rows. Switch to 3 mm / sz 3 needle and knit the pattern by following the diagram, repeat the 8 pattern rows 3 times, also garter knit the last three stitches on each side on every row as a front edge. Move onto stockinet stitch, knit 1.5 (2) 2.5 inches / 4 (5) 6 cm. Start with the slanted front edge the following way: cast off 4 st on every other row, 4 times = 38 (48) 58 st. Decrease 1 st in the front edge on every row until you are left with 24 (34) 44 st; cast off 4 stitches for the armhole when the work measures the same as the back by the armhole. Continue to decrease on every other row until you are left with 18 (22) 26 st; go on knitting without decreasing until the work measures the same as the back up by the shoulder. Cast off.

RIGHT FRONT PIECE

Cast on and knit the same way as the left front piece but mirrored.

ARMS

Cast on 41 (43) 45 st on 2.5 mm / sz 2 needle. Garter knit 3 rows. Switch to 3 mm / sz 3 needle and knit the 8 rows pattern by following the diagram; for the 2nd and 3rd size the row ends with 2 respective 2 edge stitches.

Move onto stockinet stitch and increase 1 st on each side on the 1st row, and later on every 4th row until you have 51 (53) 55 st, then on every other row until you have 63 (69) 75 st. Continue without increasing until the work measures 5.5 (6.5) 3.5 inches / 14 (16) 18 cm. Cast off.

COMPLETION

Clamp out and needle the pieces together. Place a damp cloth on top, and let it dry. Sew the shoulders together.

SURROUNDING EDGE

Cast on 80 (90) 100 st on the circular needle, have the correct size pointing against you and pick up 45 (50) 55 st along the slanted front edge on the right front piece; later 20 (22) 24 st long the neckline in the back and 45 (50) 55 st along the left front piece. Knit 5 rows with stockinet stitch, loosely cast off.

DRAWSTRING

Cast on 80 (90) 100 st on 2.5 mm / sz 2 needle, garter knit 5 rows, cast off loosely.

Sew the arms. Sew the side and arm seams; leave a hole in the upper part of the left side so that you can pull the drawstring through. Sew the loose drawstring to the side so that it starts right where the slanted front edge begins.

Lightly press down on the seams with a damp cloth.

TIPS & TRICKS

■ Skip the pattern and knit the entire garment in stockinet stitch.

■ If you would prefer that the wrap-around cardigan be buttoned together and not tied, you can skip the drawstring; just pick up stitches along the front edges and the neck in the back. Make a buttonhole on each side of the front edge and sew a button in each side.

DIAGRAM

Read the diagram from the right to the left.

Repeat the pattern's 10 st in 8 rows.
Empty box=stockinet
o= yarn over
•= purl on the right side, garter knit on the wrong side
△= slip 1 stitch, knit 2 stitches, pass slip stitch over (sl1, k2, psso)

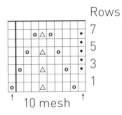

Rows

10 mesh

Hooded cardigan for the little ones

A hood is not really necessary on a baby cardigan. But it looks nice, it is fun to knit, and it could actually be practical when it is a bit cold; the small hat babies often have can be a little bit too thin.

SIZES
3–6 (6–9) 12 months

MEASUREMENTS
Length: 10 (10.5) 12 inches / 25 (27) 30 cm
Periphery: 24.5 (26.5) 28.5 inches / 62 (67) 72 cm
Arm length: 6 (7) 8 inches / 15 (17) 20 cm

MATERIALS
Yarn: 3 (4) 4 x 50 g/ 1.7 oz. thick alpaca/cotton (about 135 m/50 g/ 1.7 oz.)
Needles: 5 mm / sz 8
Other: 3 (or 5) buttons

GAUGE
16 st and 23 rows = 4x4 inch / 10x10 cm garter knit on5 mm / sz 8 needle

This garment is knitted in quite an unusual way. First the front pieces are knitted, including the front of the arms (from the bottom up). They are both placed on a joint needle and the back piece is knitted from the top down. The hood is later knitted separately and sewn on.

LEFT FRONT PIECE
Cast on 25 (27) 29 st on 5 mm / sz 8 needle and garter knit. After 5 (5.5) 6 inches / 13 (14) 15 cm, cast on 24 (24) 32 st for the arm at the beginning of the next row (from the right side). Continue garter knitting until the knit is 10.5 (11.5) 13 inches / 21 (23) 26 cm. Now cast off 7 (8) 9 st for the neck on every other row, then 3 st. You should now have 39 (44) 49 st. Knit until the work measures 25 (27)

30 st, place the stitches on a stitch holder. Finish from the wrong side.

RIGHT FRONT PIECE
Knit the same way as the left but mirrored. Knit 1 additional row to obtain identical lower edges.

BACK PIECE
Knit over the left front piece with a 5 mm / sz 8 needle (start at the wrist). Cast on 16 (18) 20 st for the neck and knit the right arm. Make sure that you do not have 2 purl- or 2 garter-knitted rows next to each other.
Now continue to garter knit until you reach the increase point for the arm. Cast off 24 (28) 32 st on each side. Continue knitting until the front and back piece are the same length. Cast off.

edge). The hood will not reach the middle front of the cardigan. Sew the buttons onto the left front edge. Fasten a piece of the yarn securely on the wrong side of the right front edge and form a loop; this is easiest with the help of a crochet hook. Align the button loops with the buttons on the other side. Do not cut the yarn but thread it through the outer edge. To fasten the loop you may sew two stitches at the same place around a knit stitch and later do the loop.

TIPS & TRICKS

■ You may also decorate the hood by placing a button right where the fold on the hood meets the neckline; this way the cardigan looks a lot more worked.

■ The garment is knitted in a rough alpaca-cotton blend and is therefore quite wool-like in its texture. If you knit it in pure cotton yarn it comes out smoother but not as warm.

Long trousers (leggings)

A pair of easily-knitted trousers like these are both practical and good-looking—a perfect gift for the expectant parent (or maybe the perfect knitting-project for the one that is expecting?) The trousers are a great project even for those who are not very familiar with knitting.

SIZES
0–3 (3–6) 6–9 months

MEASUREMENTS
Length (inseam): 7 (9) 9.5 inches / 18 (22) 24 cm
Hip periphery: 20.5 (22) 23.5 inches/ 52 (56) 60 cm

MATERIALS
Yarn: 2 (2) 3 x 50 g/ 1.7 oz. of a medium-thick yarn in a wool/ cotton blend (about 115 st/50 g/ 1.7 oz.), some leftover yarn in a different color
Needles: 3 mm / sz 3 and 4 mm / sz 6
Other: elastic band

GAUGE
22 st and 32 rows = 4x4 inch / 10x10 cm stockinet stitch on 4 mm / sz 6 needle

The trousers are knitted from the top down.

RIGHT PIECE
Cast on 54 (60) 64 st on 3 mm / sz 3 needle with the contrast color. Switch to the main color and rib knit, 1 knit, 1 purl, for 7 rows. Switch to 4 mm / sz 6 needle and stockinet stitch.

KNIT THE PANT PIECE THE FOLLOWING WAY
Row 1: Knit 10 (12) 14 st, turn and knit on the wrong side over these stitches.
Row 2: Knit 16 (18) 20 st, turn and knit on the wrong side over these stitches.
Row 3: Knit 22 (24) 26 st, turn and knit on the wrong side over these stitches. Continue to knit rows with the turn and knit 6 st more for every row until you are knitting the row with 40 (42) 44 st, turn, and knit on the wrong side over these st.

*Continue to knit with stockinet stitch over all the stitches, increase with 1 st on each side on the 5th row and later on every 10th row until you have 66 (70) 74 st. Continue without increasing until the shorter side of the work measures 7 (8) 8.5 inches / 18 (20) 21 cm. Mark with a thread on each side.

KNIT THE LEGS THE FOLLOWING WAY
Row 1: Knit 1, slip 1, knit 1, psso, garter knit up until the last 3 st, knit to st together, knit 1.
Row 2: Purl 1, Purl 2 together, purl knit up until the last 3 st, purl knit 2 together through the backloop, purl 1. Repeat these two rows 1 more time = 58 (62) 66 st.
Now decrease 1 st on each side on every 3rd row until you are left with 28 (34) 38 st. Continue without decreasing until the leg measures 7 (8) 9 inches / 18 (20) 22 cm or

wanted length, measuring from the marks. Switch to 3 mm / sz 3 needle and rib knit, 1 knit, 1 purl, for 4 rows, change to the contrast color and cast off loosely in rib stitch.

LEFT PIECE
Cast on and knit like the right piece up until the first row with a turn. Knit the row with a turn from the wrong side the following way:

Row 1: Knit 10 (12) (14) purl stitches, turn and knit straight over these st.

Row 2: Knit 16 (18) (20) purl stitches, turn and knit straight over these st.

Row 3: Knit 22 (24) 26 purl stitches, turn and knit straight over these st. Continue knitting these rows with a turn and knit 6 st more before each turn until you are knitting a row of 40 (42) 44 purl stitches, turn and knit straight over these st. Knit the rest of the left side like the right from *.

COMPLETION
Clamp the pieces out in accordance to measurements, place a damp cloth on top, and let it dry. Sew the pieces together by the markers. Sew the legs together.
Sew the elastic band in the waist and lightly press the seams.

TIPS & TRICKS
■ If you prefer a pair of trousers with straight legs just skip the decreases on the legs.
■ You can also knit a ruffled edge at the bottom of the legs if you wish to give them a more elegant feel. Ruffled edge: increase through knitting 2 st in each st, do another row of increasing like this, cast off.

Baby cardigan in tweed

This soft cardigan can have completely different looks depending on how you knit it. Here we have one variety. The different colors—lace (the pink), braided (the black), and stripes—make the variations endless.

SIZES
0–3 (3–6) 6–9 months

MEASUREMENTS
Length: 7.5 (8.5) 9.5 inches /
19 (21) 24 cm
Arm length: 6 (7) 8 inches /
15 (18) 20 cm
Width: 19.5 (21.5) 23.2
inches / 49 (54) 59 cm

MATERIALS
Yarn: all sizes 3x5 rough
tweed or wool (about 87 st /
50g)
Needles: 4.5 and 5 mm / sz 8
Other: 4 or 5 buttons

GAUGE
16 st and 23 rows on 4x5
inch / 10x10 cm stockinet
stitch on 5 mm / sz 8
needle

BACK PIECE
Cast on 42 (46) 50 st on a 4.5 mm needle. Rib knit 4 rows. Switch to 5 mm / sz 8 needle and stockinet stitch for 4 (5) 5.5 inches / 10 (12) 14 cm (excluding the rib knit). Knit the last row from the wrong side.
At the beginning of the next two rows, cast off 2 st for armholes. On the following row, from the straight side, you do another increase for the arm: * garter knit 3 st, knit 2 st together in the front stitch loop, knit up until the last 5 st of the row, knit 2 st together in the back stitch loop, garter knit 3 st. Knit the next row from the wrong side *. Repeat *-* 3 times. Now you should be left with 30 (34) 38 st. Knit stockinet stitch until the work measures 7 (8) 9 inches / 18 (20) 23 cm. Cast off 9 (10) 11 st on each side for the shoulders. Save the remaining stitches on a needle.

LEFT FRONT PIECE
Cast on 20 (22) 25 st on 4.5 mm needle. Rib knit 4 rows. Switch to 5 mm / sz 8 needle, and knit stockinet stitch for 4 (5) 5.5 inches / 10 (12) 14 cm (excluding the rib knit). Knit the last row from the wrong side.
Cast off 2 st for the armhole at the beginning of the next row that you garter knit. At the following row, from the wrong side, you continue to do decreases for the arm:
 * purl knit up until the last 5 st, purl knit 2 together, purl knit 3. Garter knit the next row *. Repeat *-* 3 times. Now you are left with 14 (16) 19 st. Continue with stockinet stitch until the work measures 6 (6.5) 8 inches / 15.5 (17) 19.5 cm.
On the following row, from the wrong side, cast off 3 st for the neck. Cast off an additional 1 st on every row 2 (3) 4 times. Now you are left with 9 (10) 12 st. Continue with stockinet stitch until the work measures 7 (8) 9 inches / 18 (20) 23 cm. Cast off all stitches.

RIGHT FRONT PIECE

Cast on and knit like the left front piece up until the first decrease for the arm, which you should now do from the wrong side. The 4 following decreases for the arm will now be done on the straight rows the following way: Garter knit 3 st, knit 2 st together in the front stitch loop, finish knitting the row. Knit the neckline mirrored against the left front piece.

ARMS

Cast on 24 (26) 28 st on 4.5 mm needle and rib knit 4 rows. Switch to 5 mm / sz 8 needle and stockinet stitch. Increase 1 st within the edge on each side on every 6th row, 3 times. Now you should have 30 (32) 34 st on the needle.
Continue until the arm measures 3.5 (5) 5.5 inches / 9 (12) 14 cm. Knit the last row from the wrong side.

Cast off 2 st at the beginning of the following 2 rows for armholes. After this, decrease another 4 times for the armhole on every other row, in other words, from the straight side the following way: * garter knit 3, knit 2 stitches together in the front stitch loop, knit up until the last 5 st, knit 2 st together in the back stitch loop, garter knit 3 st *. Now you should have 18 (20) 22 st on the needle. Now follow by casting off 3 st at the beginning of every row, 4 times. Cast off the remaining 6 (8) 10 st.

LEFT FRONT EDGE

Pick up about 35 (37) 40 st with a 4.5 mm needle (stop by the first cast off for the neck). Rib knit 5 rows, knit 1, purl 1.

RIGHT FRONT EDGE

Pick up just like you did for the left front edge, rib knit 1 row. Cast off 1 or 2 st (depending on how large the buttons are) evenly distributed for 4 buttonholes on the next row. On the following row, cast on the number of st you previously cast off. Rib knit 1 row and cast off.

NECKLINE

Sew the shoulders together. Pick up 4 st with the 4.5 mm needle at the upper side of the buttonhole edge, followed by about 20 st along the right front piece, add the saved st of the back piece, about 10 st along the left front piece and 4 st on the upper side of the front edge. Rib knit 5 rows. (If you wish you may knit 1 buttonhole at the very top on the right side.)

On the next spread you will find examples of how you can vary this cardigan.

PINK CARDIGAN WITH LACE

We have knitted this in the smallest size with a Natural Silk Aran (2 balls). The front pieces have received a zigzag lace (see diagram on p. 48); the zigzag lace can be added once or multiple times. If you only want it included once, just skip the repetition.

Row 1 (garter): * knit 2, purl 3, knit 2 together, 1 YO, garter knit 3; repeat from *.
Row 2 and every even row: purl knit.
Row 3: * knit 1, purl 3, knit 2 tog, 1 YO, knit 4; repeat from *.
Row 5: * knit 3, knit 2 tog, 1 YO, knit 5; repeat from *.
Row 7: knit 3, 1 YO, 1, sl1, k1, psso, purl 3, knit 2; repeat from *.
Row 9: knit 4, 1 YO, sl1, k1, psso, purl 3; repeat from *.
Row 11: knit 4, 1 YO, sl1, k1, psso, purl 3; repeat from *.
Row 12: purl knit.
Repeat rows 1–12.

PINKISH RED CARDIGAN

This variety is knitted in Cashsoft Aran, a mixture yarn of merino wool, microfiber, and cashmere. The buttonholes are knitted with the front piece by adding 4 extra stitches in moss stitch outside of the braid. The neckline and cuffs are also knitted in moss stitch.

Moss Stitch Garter knit 1, purl 1, the whole row, turn, and knit the next row with garter stitch from the wrong side and purl knit on the straight side. This pattern will look the same on both sides.

Braids Since braids shrink the work somewhat, 2 extra stitches are picked up at the first row after the cuff on the spot where you want to knit the braid. When the piece is ready these 2 st are then cast off in the braid on the next-to-last row before cast off for the shoulder (see diagram p.48).
BRAID 4 ST RIGHT: Lift 2 st over on a braid needle and hold it in front of the work, k2, knit the braid needle's 2 st garter stitch.
BRAID 4 ST LEFT: Lift 2 st over on a braid needle and hold it in front of the work, k2, knit the braid needle's 2 st garter stitch.

Row 1: k1, p2, k6, p2, k1.
Row 2: Garter on straight side, purl on wrong side.
Row 3: k1, p2, k2, braid 4 st left, p2, k2.
Row 4, 5, 6: As row 2.
Row 7: k1, p2, braid 4 st right, k2, p2, k2.
Row 8, 9, 10: As row 2.
Repeat rows 1–10 again.

STRIPED CARDIGAN

The cardigan, knitted in all-season cotton, has been given simple stripes over 4 rows. You can do wider or thinner stripes, but remember that if you make stripes with an uneven number of rows you should use a double point needle or circular needle, since the other color will be on the "wrong side" of the work when it is time to switch.

BLACK CARDIGAN

At the front of the arm of this cardigan in summer tweed, we've made an OXO braid. Since a braid will shrink the work somewhat we cast on 4 extra st after the rib knit at the spot where the braid was going to be. On the second-to-last row before the cast off for the shoulder we cast off the extra stitches in the braid (see diagram p.48).

O-X-O BRAID

Border with 12 st.
BRAID 4 ST RIGHT: Lift 2 st onto a braid needle and hold it on the backside of the work, k2, garter knit the 2 st on the braid needle.
BRAID 4 ST LEFT: Lift 2 st onto a braid needle and hold it in front of the work, k2, garter knit the 2 st on the braid needle.
Row 1 (garter): p2, k8, p2.
Row 2 and every row from the wrong side: Knit garter on garter and purl on purl.

Row 3: p2, braid 4 st right, braid 4 st left, p2.
Row 5: Repeat row 1.
Row 7: p2, braid 4 st left, braid 4 st right, p2.
Row 9: Repeat row 1.

Row 11: Repeat row 7.
Row 13: Repeat row 1.
Row 15: Repeat row 3.
Row 16: Repeat row 2.
Repeat rows 1–16.

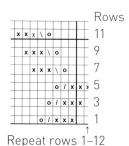

Rows
11
9
7
5
3
1

Repeat rows 1–12
and the 10 patterns

Rows
9
7
5
3
1

braided edge 12 m

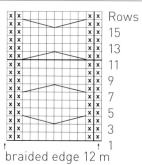

Rows
15
13
11
9
7
5
3
1

braided edge 12 m

DIAGRAM, PINK CARDIGAN WITH LACE

Read the diagram from right to left.

Empty box: stockinet stitch, in other words garter stitch on the straight side and purl stitch on the wrong side
x = purl stitch on the straight side
o = YO
\= Sl1, k1, psso
/= 2 garter stitch together

DIAGRAM, PINKISH RED CARDIGAN

Read the diagram from right to left, repeat rows 1–10.

Empty box = stockinet stitch, in other words garter stitch on the straight side and purl stitch on the wrong side
X = purl stitch on the straight side, garter stitch on the wrong side
／ = braid 4 st right, lift 2 st onto the braid needle, hold it behind the work, garter knit 2 st, garter knit the two st on the braid needle
＼ = braid 4 st left, lift 2 st onto a braid needle, hold it in front of the work, garter knit 2 st, garter knit the 2 st on the braid needle

DIAGRAM, OXO-BRAID

Read the diagram from right to left, repeat rows 1–16.

Empty box: stockinet stitch, in other words garter stitch on the straight side and purl stitch on the wrong side
x = purl stitch on the straight side, garter stitch on the wrong side
／ = braid 4 st right, lift 2 st onto the braid needle, hold it behind the work, garter knit 2 st, garter knit the two st on the braid needle
＼ = braid 4 st left, lift 2 st onto a braid needle, hold it in front of the work, garter knit 2 st, garter knit the 2 st on the braid needle

Christening gown

This christening gown in a lace pattern is fantastically beautiful and may become a nice heritage piece. This piece is not for the beginner; the rigid cotton yarn makes it somewhat harder to knit than other garments, but it is well worth the effort.

HAT (see photo on p. 47)
Size: 0–6 months

MATERIALS
Yarn: 1 ball of thin cotton yarn (140 st / 50g)
Needles: 3 mm / sz 3

GAUGE
28 st and 38 rows = 4x4 inch / 10x10 cm stockinet stitch on 3 mm / sz 3 needle
Cast on 95 st, garter knit 4 rows. Start knitting lace pattern after the diagram on p. 23 and repeat the 16 pattern rows once. Decrease 3 st, evenly distributed on the last row.

DECREASE FOR THE TOP THE FOLLOWING WAY:
Row 1: k1, k 2 tog, * k8, k2 tog; repeat from * until the last 9 st, which you garter knit.
Row 2: Purl knit.
Row 3: k1, k2 tog, * k7, k2 tog; repeat from * up until the; last 8 st, which are garter knitted.

Continue decreasing on every other row with 1 less between every decrease until you are left with 10 st. Cut the yarn and pull it through the st. Sew the hat together in the back.

SIZE
One size

MEASUREMENTS
Length: 31.5 inches / 80 cm
Periphery on top: 19 inches / 48 cm
Periphery on bottom: 43. 5 inches / 110 cm
Arm length: 5.5 inches / 14 cm

MATERIALS
Yarn: 5x50 g/ 1.7 oz. thin cotton yarn (about 140 st / 50g)
Needles: 2 and 3 mm / sz 3
Crochet needle: 2.5 mm / sz 2

GAUGE
28 st and 38 rows = 4x4 inches / 10x10 cm stockinet stitch on 3 mm / sz 3 needle

BACK PIECE
Cast on 151 st on 3 mm / sz 3 needle, garter knit 2 rows, start knitting the pattern by following the diagram; also decrease 1 st on each side on every 10th row until you are left with 101 st. Continue without decreasing until the work measures 65 st. Garter knit 2 rows, create a hole-row the following way:
* k4, k2 tog, 1 YO; repeat from * until you finish the row, complete with 5 garter st.
Garter knit 2 rows. Move onto stockinet stitch and decrease to 68 st evenly distributed over the 1st row, knit another 6 rows.

ARMHOLES
Cast off 6 st in each side. Decrease 1 st on each side on every row until you have 50 st. Knit until the armhole measures 1 inch / 2 cm.

SPLIT

Garter knit 25 st, turn, and save the other st on a needle for now. Knit each side separately. Continue with stockinet stitch until the armhole measures 4.5 inches / 11 cm.

SHOULDERS AND NECK

Cast off rows 4, 4, 5 st on every other row for the shoulder, at the same time cast off 8, 4 st for the neck. Go back to the saved st and finish the same way except mirrored.

FRONT PIECE

Cast on and knit like the back piece but without the split until the work measures 2 inches / 5 cm shorter than the back, measured form the first cast off for the shoulder.

NECK

Cast off the middle 18 st for the neck and knit each side separately. Save the other stitches on the needle. Decrease 1 st for the neck on each row until you have 13 st. Continue until the front measures the same as the back up by the shoulder. Cast off the same way you did for the back. Knit the other side the same way but mirrored.

ARMS

Cast on 46 st on 2 mm needle, garter knit 2 rows. Switch to 3 mm / sz 3 needle, increase 1 st on each side on every 4th row until you have 62 st, continue without increasing until the arm measures 5.5 inches / 14 cm.

SLEEVE CAP

Cast off 6 st in each side. Decrease 1 st in each side on every row, 4 times, then on every other row 3 times. Cast off the last 36 st.

COMPLETION

Press the pieces with a damp cloth in between. Sew the shoulders together. Crochet a row with single crochet stitch along the split.

CROCHET NECKLINE

Crochet single crochet stitch around the neck, continue by doing a scalloped edge the following way: * 1 sc, 3 ch, skip 1 st; repeat from * out the entire row.

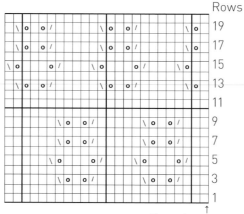

Rows

Start here
Repeat rows 1–20 and the
10 pattern stitches

DIAGRAM

Read the diagram from right to left.

Blank box= stockinet stitch
o = YO
\= sl1, k1, psso
/ = k2 together

Striped dress

The stripes give this dress a little extra touch, but it is pretty even without the stripes. The length can be varied; just remember that a longer dress is a lot harder to play in.

SIZES
6 (9) 12 (18) months

MEASUREMENTS
Periphery skirt:
34.5 (36.5) 39 (41.5) inches / 87 (93) 99 (105) cm
Periphery top:
17.5 (18) 20 (20.5) inches / 44 (46) 50 (52) cm
Length: 14.5 (15.5) 17 (18) inches / 37 (40) 43 (46) cm

MATERIALS
Yarn: a thin wool yarn (about 160 st/50 g/ 1.7 oz.)
Color A: 2 (2)2 (3) balls light pink
Color B: 2 (2) 2 (3) balls gray
Color C: 1 ball dark pink
Needles: 2.5 mm and 3 mm / sz 3
Other: 1 button

GAUGE
28 st and 40 rows = 4x4 inch / 10x10 cm stockinet stitch on 3 mm / sz 3 needle

BACK PIECE
Cast on 124 (132) 140 (148) st on 3 mm / sz 3 needle with color C. Stockinet stitch 4 rows. Make a row of eyelet holes the following way: * k2 tog, 1 YO; repeat from * the entire row. Purl knit 1 row. Continue in stockinet stitch and knit stripes that are 2 rows wide with color B and A until the work measures 10 (10.5) 11.5 (12) inches / 25 (27) 29 (31) cm. Decrease for the waist the following way:
Knit two and two together = 62 (66) 70 (74) st.
Switch to thinner needles; rib knit stripes, k1, p1, for 8 rows. Switch to bamboo needles and stockinet stitch, continue knitting until the work measures 10.5 (11.5) 12 (13) inches / 27 (29) 31 (33) cm.

ARMHOLES
Cast off 3, 1 (3,3,3) 3,2,1 (4,2,1) st in each side on every other row for the armholes = 54 (56) 58 (60) st. Knit 1.5 inches / 4 cm.

SPLIT
Knit 27 (28) 29 (30) st. Turn and save the other stitches on the needle for now. Knit each side separately. Continue with the stripes, but knit the outer two st against the split with garter stitch so that the edge will not roll inwards. Knit until the work measures 4 (4.5) 5 (5) inches / 10 (11) 12 (13) cm after the decrease for the armhole.

SHOULDERS AND NECK
Cast off 6,6,6 (6,6,6) 7,6,6 (7,6,6) st on each side on every other row. At the same time as the second casting off for the shoulder cast off 4,5 (5,5) 5,5 (6,5) st for the neck on every other row. Go back to the saved stitches and finish like you did on the first side but mirrored.

FRONT PIECE

Cast on and knit like the back piece until the work measures 2.5 (3) 3 (3.5) inches / 6 (7) 8 (9) cm after the cast off for the armhole.

NECK

Cast off the middle 12 (14) 14 (16) st for the neck. Knit each side separately and decrease 1,1,1 st on every other row for the neck. Continue without decreasing until the front piece measures the same as the back up by the first cast off for the shoulder. Cast off the same way

you did for the back piece. Knit the other side the same way but mirrored.

ARMS

Cast on 36 (40) 44 (48) st on a 2.5 mm / sz 2 needle with color C. Knit a scalloped edge the same way you did for the back piece. Switch to 3 mm / sz 3 needle, knit stripes in stockinet stitch, increase to 62 (66) 70 (74) st evenly distributed on the first row. Knit until the arm measures 1.5 (2) 2 (2) inches / 4 (5) 5 (5) cm.

ARM CAP

Cast off 3,2,2 st on each side on every other row. Now decrease 1 st on every other row 8 (9) 10 (11) times. Then cast off 2,3,4 st on each side on every other row. Cast off the remaining stitches.

COMPLETION

Press or clamp out the pieces according to the measurements, and cover with a damp cloth. Sew the shoulders together. Start by the split and pick up 66 (72) 78 (84) st with a 2.5 mm / sz 2 needle evenly distributed around the neck. Make a row of eyelet holes the same way as before, knit 4 rows with stockinet stitch, cast off loosely. Sew the side and arm seams. Sew the arms onto the shoulders. Fold the edges inwards around the row of eyelet holes and fasten from the inside. Lightly press down on the scalloped edge and the seams. Sew a small button loop up by the neck and sew a button on the other side.

Dress with yoke

A beautiful Christmas dress that is knitted with only garter and purl stitches; in other words, you can knit this very quickly. Well-chosen buttons take this dress from a simple everyday dress to a nice evening gown.

SIZES
6 (9) 12 (18) months

MEASUREMENTS
Periphery skirt:
33.5 (36.5) 39 (41.5) inches /
85 (93) 99 (105) cm
Periphery top:
16 (16.5) 17.5 (18.5) inches /
40 (42) 44 (47) cm
Length: 12.5 (14) 16 (17.5)
inches / 32 (36) 40 (44) cm

MATERIALS
Yarn: 4 (4) 5 (6) x 5 g of a
thin cotton yarn
(about 140 st/50 g/ 1.7 oz.)
Needles: 2.5 and 3 mm / sz 3
Other: 3 small buttons

GAUGE
30 st and 38 rows = 4x4 inch /
10x10 cm stockinet stitch on
3 mm / sz 3 needle

BACK PIECE
Cast on 124 (132) 140 (148) st on
2.5 mm needle. Knit simple moss
stitch for 5 rows. Switch to 3 mm /
sz 3 needle and stockinet stitch,
knit until the work measures 8 (9)
9.5 (11) inches / 20 (22) 24 (28) cm.

SPLIT
Knit 62 (66) 70 (74) st, turn, and purl
knit 1 row. Save the other stitches
on a spare needle for now. Kit each
side separately. Knit 2 rows.

ARMHOLES
Cast off 2 st in the armhole side,
knit 1 row. Decrease 1 st for the
armhole on every other row, 4
times = 56 (60) 64 (68) st.
Knit two and two together over the
next row = 28 (30) 32 (34) st. Garter
knit 3 rows to mark the beginning of
the yoke. Continue without decreasing until the work measures 12
(13.5) 15 (16.5) inches / 30 (34) 38
(42) cm; finish on the straight side.

NECK
Cast off 10 (12) 12 (13) st for the
neck, finish knitting the row. Knit
1 row. Cast off another 3 st for
the neck at the beginning of the
next row. Knit 2 rows, cast off the
last 15 (15) 17 (18) st. Go back to
the saved stitches and finish like
you did on the first side but
mirrored.

FRONT PIECE
Cast on and knit like the back
piece (without the split) up until
the armhole.

ARMHOLE
Cast off 2 st on each side, then
decrease 1 st on each side on
every other row, 4 times = 112
(120) 128 (126) st. Garter knit 3
rows to mark the beginning of the
yoke. Continue without decreasing
until the work measures 10.5
(11.5) 13 (15.5) inches / 27 (29) 33
(39) cm.

NECK

Cast off the middle 14 (16) 18 (20) st for the neck, knit each side separately. Decrease 1 st for the neck on each row until you are left with 15 (15) 17 (18) st. Continue without decreasing until the work measures the same as the back up by the shoulder. Cast off.
Go back to the saved stitches and knit the same way as the first side but mirrored.

ARMS

Cast on 45 (49) 53 (57) st on 2.5 mm / sz 2 needle, rib knit, k1, p1 for 5 (7) 7 (9) rows.
Switch to 3 mm / sz 3 needle and stockinet stitch, at the same time increase 10 st evenly distributed over the first row = 55 (59) 63 (67) st. Now increase 1 st on each side on every other row until you have 65 (69) 73 (77) st, knit 3 (3) 5 (5) rows without increasing.

ARMHOLES

Cast off 2 st on each side. Decrease 1 st on each side on every other row until you are left with 55 (59) 63 (67) st.
Now decrease over the entire row the following way:
Garter knit 2 st, * k2 tog, k4; repeat from * the rest of the row.

Cast off on the next row.

COMPLETION

Clamp out or press the pieces after the measurements, and cover with a damp cloth.
Sew the shoulders together. Mark for 3 buttons on the left side of the split (let the third button get as close to the neck as possible).

SPLIT

Pick evenly distributed st from the straight side along the split with a 2.5 mm / sz 2 needle. Garter knit 1 row. Next row: Garter knit, and at the same time make 3 buttonholes on the right side directly opposite

of the markings by knitting 2 st together, 1 YO. Cast off with garter stitches on the next row.

NECKLINE

Pick up about 60 (63) 67 (71) st evenly distributed around the neck with a 2.5 mm / sz 2 needle. Make a scalloped edge the following way:
Cast off 3 st, * cast on 2 new stitches (see knitted cast on p.112), cast off 5 st; repeat from * out the entire row.

Sew the side and arm seams. Wrinkle the arm cap together so that the arm fits in the armhole. Fasten the arms to the dress. Gently press down on the seams.

Warm baby blanket

A cozy baby blanket that works just as well to wrap the baby as it does as an extra cover in the stroller or bed. If you wish to make the blanket especially simple, skip the edge; in that case the whole blanket is garter knitted back and forth.

MEASUREMENT
About 43.5x49 inches / 110x125 cm excluding the edge

MATERIALS
Yarn: 12x50 g / 1.7 oz. of a medium-thick wool yarn (about 125 st/50 g/ 1.7 oz.)
Needles: circular needle 3.5 mm / sz 4 mm, 31.5 inches long / 80 cm

GAUGE
22 st and 40 rows= 4x4 inch / 10x10 cm garter knit on 3.5 mm / sz 4 mm needle

Cast on about 350 st (the exact number is not important since the blanket is knitted solely in garter knit) on a 3.5 mm / sz 4 mm circular needle. Garter knit back and forth until the work measures about 39.5 inches / 100 cm.

EDGE
The edge is knitted separately and then sewn on afterwards. Knit in 4 lengths, one for each side. You may also knit the edge in 1 long piece. In that case, be careful to not stretch it out around the corners; it should rather be squeezed together so that the corners will not fold.
Cast on 6 st.

Row 1 (garter): k1, 1 YO, k2 tog, 1 YO, k2.
Row 2 and all rows on the wrong side: Garter knit.
Row 3: k3, 1 YO, k2 tog, 1 YO, k2.
Row 5: k2, 1 YO, k2 tog, 1 YO, k2 tog, 1 YO, k2.
Row 7: k3, 1 YO, k2 tog, 1 YO, k2 tog, 1 YO, k2.
Row 8: Cast off 4 st, garter knit the rest of the row.
Repeat rows 1–8.

TIPS & TRICKS

■ In works where you need to knit a large number of stitches on each row we recommend using a circular needle since the weight of the knitting may otherwise be straining on both shoulders and wrists.

■ This blanket is also very pretty in a single or double moss stitch. In single moss stitch you knit purl stitches on the straight side; in double moss stitch you do the follwing:

R1: * k2, p2, repeat from *
R2: garter stitch on straight side, purl stitch on wrong side
R3: * p2, k2, repeat from *
R4: purl stitch on the wrong side, garter stitch on the straight side
Repeat rows 1–4.

■ If you prefer not to knit the entire blanket in one large piece you can divide it in smaller squares and sew them together. You may even sew the squares together with large stitches in a contrasting color so the seams become a decorative element.

■ The edge can be knitted in the same color or shade, or in a completely different color.

Stroller blanket

The vivid colors work well with modern strollers. The blanket is knitted in squares; therefore, you may easily vary the size. A warm knitted wool blanket is unbeatable; if you want a softer underside you can line it with thin fleece lining.

MEASUREMENTS
One square measures
7.5x7.5 inches / 19x19 cm

MATERIALS
Yarn: 8x50 g/ 1.7 oz. of a thick yarn (about 87 st/50 g/ 1.7 oz.) in the following colors:
Color A: 4 balls dark gray
Color B: 4 balls wine-red
Needles: 4.5 mm

GAUGE
8 st and 38 rows = 4x4 inch / 10x10 cm garter knit on 4.5 mm needle.

Squares (make 12 of these)
Cast on 105 st on 4.5 st needle with color A.
Row 1 and every odd row (wrong side): Garter knit with the same color as the previous row.
Row 2: k2 tog, (k23, k3 tog) 3 times, k23, k2 tog = 97 st.
Row 4: k2 tog, (k21, k3 tog) 3 times, k21, k2 tog = 89st.
Row 6: k2 tog, (k19, k3 tog) 3 times, k 19, k2 tog = 81 st.
Change to color B (after row 7)
Row 8: k2 tog, (k17, k3 tog) 3 times, k17, k2 tog = 73 st.
Row 10: k1 tog, (k15, k3 tog) 3 times, k15, k2 tog = 65 st.
Row 12: k2 tog, (k13, k3 tog) 3 times, k13, k2 tog = 57 st.
Row 14: k2 tog, (k11, k3 tog) 3 times, k11, k2 tog = 49 st.
Switch back to color A after row 15.
Row 16: k2 tog, (k9, k3 tog) 3 times, k9, k2 tog = 41 st.
Row 18: k2 tog, (k7, k3 tog) 3 times, k7, k7 tog = 33 st.
Row 20: k2 tog, (k5, k3 tog) 3 times, k5, 2 tog = 25 st.
Row 22: k2 tog, (k3, k3 tog) 3 times, k3, k2 tog = 17 st.
Row 24: k2 tog, (k1, k3 tog) 3 times, k1, k2 tog = 9 st.
Row 24: Garter knit.
Cut the yarn and thread it through the remaining 9 st. Pull hard so that it fastens, sew the sides together so that you have a square. Do another 11 squares the exact same way; make 5 squares that start with color A and 5 squares that start with color B.

COMPLETION
Clamp the squares out in accordance to the measurements, and cover with a damp cloth. Sew the squares together so that you have 3 squares in width and 4 squares in length.

Braided sweater

A warm sweater to pull on when cold weather suddenly arrives. The braids are easy to learn; the sweater looks significantly more complicated than it is.

SIZES
2 (4) 6 (8) 10 years

MEASUREMENTS
Length: 12.5 (15) 16.5 (18) 20 inches / 32 (38) 42 (46) 48 cm
Periphery: 25 (25.5) 28 (30) 34 inches / 64 (65) 72 (77) 86 cm
Arm length: 9.5 (11) 12.5 (15) 16.5 inches / 24 (28) 32 (38) 42 cm

MATERIALS
Yarn: 8 (10) 11 (12) 14 x50 g / 1.7 oz. of a medium-thick cotton yarn (about 85 st / 50 g / 1.7 oz.)
A piece of left-over yarn in a contrasting color (optional)
Needles: 3.5 mm / sz 4 mm and 4 mm / sz 6 and cable needle

GAUGE
22 st and 28 rows = 4x4 inch / 10x10 cm patterned on 4 mm / sz 6 needle

BACK PIECE
Cast on 66 (72) 78 (84) 90 st on a 3.5 mm / sz 4 mm needle with the contrast yarn. Switch to the main color and rib knit, k2, p2, for 1.5 (1.5) 2.5 (3) 3 inches / 4 (4) 6 (7) 7 cm, also increase to 76 (78) 86 (94) 104 st on the last rib-knit row. Switch to 4 mm / sz 6 needle and start knitting the pattern after the diagram until the work measures 7 (8.5) 9.5 (11) 11.5 inches / 18 (22) 25 (28) 29 cm.
Set up the pattern the following way:
Size 2 years: 1 edge st, p2, repeat rapport 4 times, finish with 6 moss stitches, p2, 1 edge st.
Size 4 years: 1 edge st, 1 stockinet stitch, p2, repeat rapport 4 times, finish with 6 moss stitches, p2, 1 stockinet st, 1 edge st.
Size 6 years: 1 edge st, 5 stockinet st, p2, repeat rapport 4 times, finish with 6 moss st, p2, 5 stockinet st, 1 edge st.
Size 8 years: 1 edge st, 1 moss st, p2, braid over 6 st, p2, repeat rapport 5 times, 1 moss st, 1 edge st.
Size 10 years: 1 edge st, repeat rapport 6 times, 6 moss st, 1 edge st.

ARMHOLES
Cast off 4 st on each side, then decrease 1 st on each side on every row 5 (6) 6 (7) 7 times = 58 (58) 66 (72) 82. Continue pattern until the back piece measures 12.5 (15) 16.5 (18) 20 inches / 32 (38) 42 (46) 48 cm altogether.
Cast off.

TIPS & TRICKS

■ The sweater may also be knitted in a denim yarn. The yarn will bleach and shrink after washing, just like jeans. The braid pattern gives the garment a nice look even when it is quite worn. The yarn only shrinks the length; add 4 cm on the front and back piece and 1 (1) 1 (1.5) 1.5 inches / 2 (3) 3 (4) 4 cm on the arms.

repeat 16 st.

rows
5
3
1

DIAGRAM

Read the diagram from the right to the left.

[square] =garter stitch on the straight side, purl stitch on the wrong side

x =purl on the straight side, garter on the wrong side

[three squares and slashes] =braid 6 st right: lift 3 st onto a cable needle, hold this behind the work, k3, garter knit the st on the cable needle

- = the arm's braided edge over 26 st

FRONT PIECE

Cast on and knit the front piece like the back until the work measures 2 (2) 2.5 (2.5) 2.5 inches / 5 (5) 6 (6) 6 cm shorter when measured from the shoulder.

NECK

Cast off the middle when 20 (22) 24 (24) 24 st for the neck and knit each side separately. Save the other st on a spare needle for now. Decrease 1 st for the neck on each row 3 times, then on every other row until you are left with 8 (10) 12 (14) 16 st. Continue until the front measures the same as the back up by the shoulder, cast off. Knit the other side the same way but mirrored.

Cast on 36 (38) 40 (42) 44 st on 3.5 mm / sz 4 mm needle with the contrast yarn. Switch to the main color and rib knit, k2, p2, for 2 inches / 5 cm. Increase to 40 (44) 48 (52) 56 st evenly distributed over the last rib-knit row. Switch to 4 mm / sz 6 needle and start knitting the pattern after the diagram. Set up the pattern the following way: 7 (9) 11 (13) 15 moss st, p2, 6 st braid, p2, 6 moss st, p2, 6 st braid, p 2, finish the row with moss stitch. Continue this pattern and also increase 1 st on each side of every 4th row until you have 56 (68) 62 (64) 55 st.
Continue without increasing until the arm measures 9.5 (11) 12.5 (7.5) 8.5 inches / 24 (28) 32 (38) 42 cm or the wanted length.

ARM CAP

Cast off 4 st on each side, then 1 st on each side on every row, 7 times, cast off the remaining 34 (36) 40 (42) 44 st.

COMPLETION

Clamp the pieces out according to the measurements and cover with a damp cloth. Let it dry.

NECKLINE

Sew the right shoulder together. Pick 86 (88) 90 (90) 96 st evenly distributed around the neck from the straight side with a 3.5 mm / sz 4 mm needle. Rib knit, k2, p2, for 1.5 (1.5) 2 (2) 2 inches / 4 (4) 5 (5) 5 cm cast of rib knit. Sew the left shoulder together and the short side of the neck. Sew the side and arm seams together. Sew the arms to the sweater.

V-neck with joyful stripes

Joyful colors are irresistible on children. This sweater is quick to knit; the only thing that may take some time is fastening all of the threads. When it is all finished this sweater will become a favorite with both girls and boys.

SIZES
2 (4) 6 (8) 10 years

MEASUREMENTS
Length: 13.5 (16) 17.5 (18) 19 inches / 34 (40) 44 (46) 48 cm
Periphery: 24.5 (26) 28.5 (31) 33 inches / 62 (66) 72 (78) 84 cm
Arm length: 9.5 (11) 12.5 (15) 16.5 inches / 24 (28) 32 (38) 42 cm

MATERIALS
Yarn: a medium-thick cotton yarn (about 85 st / 50 g / 1.7 oz.)
Yarn colors:
Color A, marine blue: 2 (2) 3 (4) 5 balls
Color B, red: 1 (1) 2 (2) 2 balls
Color C, turquoise: 1 (1) 2 (2) 2 balls
Color D, lime green: 1 (1) 2 (2) 2 balls
Color E, nature white: 1 (1) 2 (2) 2 balls
Color F, beige: 1 (1) 2 (2) 2 balls
Needles: 3 mm / sz 3 and 4 mm / sz 6

GAUGE
20 st and 28 rows= 4x4 inch / 10x10 cm stockinet stitch on 4 mm / sz 6 needle

STRIPE PATTERN
Row 1–4: Color A.
Row 5: Color E.
Row 6–7: Color D.
Row 8: Color E.
Row 9–12: Color A.
Row 13: Color E.
Row 14–15: Color F.
Row 16: Color E.
Row 17–20: Color A.
Row 21: Color E.
Row 22–23: Color B.
Row 24: Color E.
Row 25–28: Color A.
Row 29: Color E.
Row 30–31: Color C.
Row 32: Color E.
Repeat these 32 rows; this creates the striped pattern.

BACK PIECE
Cast on 66 (70) 74 (78) 84 st on 3 mm / sz 3 needle with color C. Switch to color A, rib knit, k1, p2, for 1.5 (1.5) 2 (2.5) 3 inches / 4 (4) 5 (6) 7 cm. Switch to 4 mm / sz 6 needle and stockinet stitch, start knitting stripes in accordance with the pattern. Continue with stripes until the work measures 8 (9.5) 10.5 (11) 11.5 inches / 20 (24) 27 (28) 29 cm.

ARMHOLES
Cast off 3 st on each side. Decrease 1 st on each side on every row 3 (3) 3 (1) 1 times, then on every other row 2 (2) 2 (3) 4 times = 50 (54) 58 (64) 68 st. * Continue without decreases until the back piece measures 13 (15.5) 17 (17.5) 18.5 inches / 33 (39) 43 (45) 47 cm.

SHOULDERS AND NECK
Cast off the middle 28 (32) 34 (38) 40 st, knit each side separately. Save the other st on a needle. Cast off 3 st against the neck at the beginning of the next row. Cast off 4,4

(4,4) 4,5 (5,5) 5,6 st on every other row for the shoulder.
Knit the other side the same way but mirrored.

FRONT PIECE

Cast on and knit like the back piece up until the *.

V-NECK

Knit 24 (26) 28 (31) 33 st, turn and save the other st on a stitch holder or a spare needle.
Knit each side separately.
Decrease 1 st for the V-neck on every row until you are left with 8 (8) 9 (10) 11 st, continue without more decreases until the front measures the same as the back up by the shoulder, cast off the same way you did for the back.
Go back to the saved st, move the middle 2 stitches onto a safety pin, knit the other side like the first but mirrored.

ARMS

Cast on 34 (36) 38 (40) 42 st on 3 mm / sz 3 needle with color D. Change to color A and rib knit, k2, p2, for 2.5 inches / 6 cm. Switch to 4 mm / sz 6 needle and striped pattern, increase 1 st on each side on every 6th (6th) 6th (8th) 8th row until you have 52 (54) 56 (58) 60 st, continue without increasing until the arm measures 9.5 (11) 12.5 (15) 16.5 inches / 24 (28) 32 (38) 42 cm or the wanted length.

ARM CAP

Cast off 3 st on each side.
Decrease 1 st on each side on every row 5 times, then on every other row until you are left with 28 st, then on every row 7 times.

COMPLETION

Clamp the pieces out in accordance with the measurements. Cover with a damp cloth and let it dry. Sew the right shoulder together.
Work from the straight side, pick with color A and 3 mm / sz 3 needle around the neck the following way: Pick 30 (34) 38 (42) 46 st along the left side on the front neck, place a yarn marker on the needle, garter knit the saved 2 st, place another mark on the needle, pick up 30 (34) 38 (42) 46 st along the back neck = 92 (104) 116 (128) 136 st. Rib knit back and forth, k2, p2.
Rib knit row 1 (wrong side): p2, (k2, p2) repeat up until 2 st before the marked st, Sl1, k1, psso, p2, (the marked st), k2 tog, finish the row in rib knit.

Rib knit row 2: k2, (p2, k2) repeat up until 2 st before the marked st, p2 st through the back stitch loop, k2 (the marked st), p2 tog, knit the rest of the row in rib knit.
Continue decreasing 1 stitch on each side around the marked st the same way, knit 5 rows altogether, switch to color B and cast off in rib knit. Decrease 1 st on each side around the marked st the same way as before. Sew the other shoulder together and the short side of the neckline.
Sew side and arm seams together. Sew the arms to the sweater. Gently press down on the seams.

TIPS & TRICKS
■ This is a classic V-neck sweater, and may of course be knitted in one single color as well.

Fisherman's rib raglan sweater

The same sweater, but in two variations. The sweater is knitted with half-fisherman's rib which makes soft, wonderful and warm garments that work in all occasions. It is very hard to pick up dropped stitches so the best thing here is to make sure not to drop any . . .

SIZES
2 (4) 6 (8) 10 years

MEASUREMENTS
Length: 13.5 (15) 17.5 (18) 20 inches / 34 (38) 44 (46) 50 cm
Periphery: 26 (27.5) 30.5 (32.5) 34 inches / 66 (70) 78 (82) 86 cm
Arm length: 10 (12.5) 13.5 (15) 16.5 inches / 26 (32) 34 (38) 42 cm

MATERIALS
Yarn: 5 (7) 8 (9) 10 x 50 g / 1.7 oz. of a medium–thick wool yarn (about 115 st /50 g / 1.7 oz.)
Needles: 3 mm / sz 3 and 4 mm / sz 6, a stitch holder

GAUGE
20 st and 44 rows = 4x4 inch / 10x10 cm fisherman's rib on 4mm needle

PATTERN
Row 1: Garter knit.
Row 2: k1, * k1 in the row underneath the next st, p1; repeat from * out.
Repeat 1 and 2.

BACK PIECE
Cast on 65 (69) 77 (83) 87 st on 3 mm / sz 3 needle, rib knit, k1, p1, for 1.5 (1.5) 2 (2) 2.5 inches / 4 (4) 5 (5) 6 cm.
Switch to 4 mm / sz 6 needle and start knitting pattern (see above) until the work measures 5 (7) 9 (10) 11 inches / 13 (18) 22 (25) 28 cm.

RAGLAN
Continue with pattern, cast off 2 st on each side. Now decrease 1 st on each side on every other and every 4th row until you are left with 23 (25) 27 (27) 29 st; the armhole should measure about 5.5 (6) 7 (7) 7.5 inches / 14 (15) 17 (18) 19 cm.

NECK
Continue decreasing for raglan. Lift the middle 7 (7) 9 (11) 11 st on a stitch holder, knit each side separately. Cast off 3,2 (3,2) 4,3 (4,3) 4,3 st against the neck on every other row. Continue decreasing for raglan until you have 2 st left, knit these together and pull through the yarn.
Knit the other side the same way but mirrored.

FRONT PIECE

Cast on and knit like the back until you are left with 27 (29) 31 (31) 33 st after the decrease to raglan.

NECK

Continue decreasing for raglan, lift the middle 7 (7) 9 (11) 11 st onto a stitch holder, knit each side separately. Cast off 3 (3) 4 (4) 4 st for the neck, decrease 1 st on each row 2 (2) 3 (3) 3 times, continue decreasing for raglan until you are left with 2 st, knit these two st together and pull through the yarn. Knit the other side the same way but mirrored.

ARMS

Cast on 36 (38) 40 (40) 42 st on 3 mm / sz 3 needle, rib knit, k1, p1, for 1.5 (1.5) 2 (2) 2.5 inches / 4 (4) 5 (5) 6 cm. Switch to 4 mm / sz 6 needle and start knitting the following pattern. Increase 1 st in every side on every 10th row until there are 52 (56) 62 (70) 76 st. Continue without increasing until the arm measures 10 (12.5) 14 (15) 16.5 inches / 26 (32) 36 (38) 42 cm.

RAGLAN

Continue with pattern, cast off 2 st on each side. Decrease 1 st on each side on every other row and every 4th row until you have as many raglan decreases as you have on the front and back pieces. Save the remaining st on a cast off needle.

COMPLETION

Clamp the pieces out in accordance with the measurements, cover with a moist cloth, and let it dry. Sew all of the raglan seams together, except the right back.

NECKLINE

Pick up with 3 mm / sz 3 needle form the straight side about 65 (69) 69 (73) 77 st around the neck (including the saved st).
Rib knit, k1, p1, for 1.5 (2) 2 (2) 2.5 inches / 4 (5) 5 (5) 6 cm, cast off in rib knit. Sew the last raglan seam together. Fold the collar in half inwards and sew fixed, or you may let the collar fold outwards as a polo-collar. Sew the side and arm seams. Gently press the seams.

Pippi sweater

The world's strongest girl often wore a white sweater with red and blue stripes. The Pippi sweater is quick to knit and it gives an energy boost to anyone who sees it. The ties may be white, blue, red, or in two different colors.

SIZES
2 (4) 6 (8) 10

MEASUREMENTS
Length: 14 (16.5) 18 (20.5) 23 inches / 36 (42) 46 (52) 58 cm
Periphery: 24.5 (26) 28.5 (31) 33 inches / 62 (66) 72 (78) 84 cm
Arm length: 9.5 (11) 12.5 (15) 16.5 inches / 24 (28) 32 (38) 42 cm

MATERIALS
Yarn: a medium-thick wool yarn (about 115 st / 50 g/ 1.7 oz.)
Colors:
Base color (bc), nature white: 5 (6) 7 (8) 9 x 50 g / 1.7 oz.
Red: 1 (1) 1 (1) 1 x 50 g / 1.7 oz.
Blue: 1 (1) 1 (1) 1 x 50 g/ 1.7 oz.
Needles: 3.5 mm / sz 4 mm and 4 mm / sz 6, circular needle 3.5 mm / sz 4 mm, 20 inch / 40 cm long, opt. Double-pointed needle 3.5 mm / sz 4

GAUGE
23 st and 28 rows = 4x4 inch / 10x10 cm stockinet stitch on 4 mm / sz 6 needle

STRIPES
Row 1: Every other st in base color and every other st in pattern color.
Row 2-3: Pattern color.
Row 4: Every other st in basic color and every other st in pattern color (take care that the pattern color is knitted above the same st as in row 1).

BACK PIECE
Cast on 76 (80) 86 (92) 100 st with bc on a 3.5 mm / sz 4 mm needle, garter knit for 5 rows, switch to 4 mm / sz 6 needle and stockinet stitch. Knit 2 rows in the basic color, and then knit the first stripe. Knit 14 rows of base color between each stripe.
Knit until the work measures 14 (15.5) 18 (20.5) 22.8 inches / 36 (42) 46 (52) 58 cm. Cast off the middle 22 (24) 26 (28) 30 st for the neck, knit separately. Save the other st on the needle for now, cast off an additional 3 st against the neck. Cast off the remaining 24 (25) 27 (29) 32 st

for the shoulder. Knit the other side the same way but mirrored.

FRONT PIECE
Cast on and knit like the back until the work measures 4 (4.5) 4.5 (5.5) 5.5 inches / 10 (12) 12 (14) 14 cm shorter than the back piece measures from the shoulder.

SPLIT
Knit 37 (39) 42 (45) 49 st, turn and knit each side separately. Continue in pattern until the front is 1.5 (1.5) 2 (2) 2.5 inches / 4 (4) 5 (5) 6 cm shorter than the back measures from the shoulder.

NECK
Cast off on every other row and in turns; 5,3,2 (6,3,2) 7,3,2 (8,3,2) 9,3,2 st for the neck, then decrease on every other row until you are left with 24 (25) 27 (29) 32 st for the shoulder; cast off when the front measures the same as the back.

Go back to the saved st and cast off the middle 2 st; knit the same way as the first side but mirrored.

ARMS

Cast on 48 (50) 52 (54) 56 st with bc on 3.5 mm / sz 4 mm needle and garter knit 5 rows. Switch to 4 mm / sz 6 needle and stockinet stitch, make the stripes the same way you did for the front and back piece. Increase on every 6th row until you have 66 (72) 78 (86) 96 st, knit until the arm measures 24 (28) 32 (38) 42 st, cast off loosely.

COMPLETION

Clamp the pieces out in accordance with the measurements, cover with a damp cloth, and let it dry.

Sew the shoulders together. Use the circular needle and pick up evenly distributed stitches around the neck and split from the straight side, garter knit 1 row. Cast off with garter stitches.

Sew the arms to the sweater; make sure that the middle of the arm is aligned with the middle of the shoulder. Sew side and arm seams. Gently press down on the seams.

TIES (make 2 in optional color)
Cast on 4 st on the circular needles or double-pointed needle, garter knit 4 st, move the st onto the other end of the needle, pull the yarn hard on the wrong side, garter knit the 4 st once more, repeat until the tie measures about 8 inches / 20 cm or the preferred length. Cast off.
Sew the ties to the neckline on each side of the split.

Cardigan with crocheted flowers

This cardigan is a classic shape. The thing that makes it unique are the crochet flowers which can also be made in one color for a quieter look. The cardigan can also be decorated with embroidery.

SIZES
2 (4) 6 (8) years

MEASUREMENTS
Length: 13.5 (15) 16.5 (18) inches / 34 (38) 42 (46) cm
Periphery: 25 (27) 28.5 (31) inches / 64 (68) 72 (78) cm
Arm length: 9.5 (11) 12.5 (15) inches / 24 (28) 32 (38) cm

MATERIALS
Yarn: 4 (5) 6 (7) x 50 g / 1.7 oz. of a medium-thick wool yarn (about 115 st /50 g / 1.7 oz.) and left-over yarn for the crochet flowers
Needles: 3 mm / sz 3 and 4 mm / sz 6
Crochet needle: 3.5 mm / sz 4 mm
Other: 5 (5) 7 (7) buttons

GAUGE
22 st and 30 rows = 4x4 inch / 10x10 cm inches stockinet stitch on 4 mm / sz 6 needle

BACK PIECE
Cast on 71 (75) 79 (85) st on 3 mm / sz 3 needle, knit moss stitch for 3 rows. Switch to 4 mm / sz 6 needle and stockinet stitch, knit until the work measures 7.5 (9) 10 (11.5) inches / 19 (22) 26 (29) cm.

ARMHOLES
Cast off 4 st on each side. Decrease 1 st on each side on every row 1 (1) 3 (3) times, then every other row until there are 53 (57) 61 (67) st. Continue without decreasing until the work measures 13 (14.5) 16 (18) inches/ 33 (37) 41 (45) cm. Cast off the middle 15 (15) 17 (19) st for the neck and knit each side separately. Save the other stitches on the needle for now. Cast off 4 st against the neck at the beginning of the next row. Cast off 15 (17) 18 (20) st for the shoulder. Go back to the saved st and finish the same way but mirrored.

LEFT FRONT PIECE
Cast on 41 (43) 45 (47) st on 3 mm / sz 3 needle, moss stitch 6 rows. Switch to 4 mm / sz 6 needle and stockinet stitch, continue knitting the outer 5 st in moss stitch for the front edge, knit until the work measures the same as the back up by the cast off for the shoulder; finish from the wrong side.

ARMHOLES
Cast off 4 st for the armhole. Decrease 1 st on every row 1 (1) 3 (3) times, then on every other row until there are 28 (30) 34 (37) st. Continue in stockinet and moss stitch until the front piece is 2 (2) 2.5 (3) inches / 5 (5) 6 (7) cm shorter than the back measured from the first decrease for the shoulder.

NECK
Knit the front edge 5 st in moss stitch and move them onto a safety pin. Cast off 4,3 st for the neck on

every other row, decrease 1 st for the neck on every other row until there are 15 (17) 18 (20) st. Continue until the front measures the same as the back up by the shoulder, cast off. Mark for 4 (4) 6 (6) buttons on the moss stitch edge, situate the first button about 1 inch / 1 cm above the bottom edge. The last button should be on the neckline which you will knit later on with the rest evenly distributed in between.

RIGHT FRONT PIECE

Cast on 41 (43) 45 (47) st on 3 mm / sz 3 needle, knit 6 rows with moss stitch, make a buttonhole on the 4th row: knit 2 st moss stitch, 2 st together, 1 YO, 2 moss stitch. Make the other button holes directly opposite the marks for buttons.
Switch to 4 mm / sz 6 needle and knit the rest of the right front piece like the left but mirrored.

ARMS

Cast on 41 (43) 45 (47) st on 3 mm / sz 3 needle, knit 6 rows in moss stitch. Switch to 4 mm / sz

6 needle and stockinet stitch, also increase on each side (on the inside of the outer 2 st) on the 3rd row and later on every 6th (6th) 8th (8th) row until there are 55 (57) 59 (61) st, continue without increasing until the arm measures 9.5 (11) 12.5 (14) inches / 24 (28) 32 (36) cm.

ARM CAP

Cast off 4 st on each side. Decrease 1 st on each side on every row 3 times, then on every other row 6 (6) 2 (2) times = 29 (31) 41 (43) st. On the two largest sizes you now decrease on every 4th row until there are 35 (37) st. Now decrease 1 st on each side on every row until there are 21 (21) 23 (23) st left, cast off all the st.

COMPLETION

Clamp the pieces out in accordance with the measurements, cover with a damp cloth and let it dry.
Sew the shoulders together.

NECKLINE

Pick up the saved 5 st from the straight side, with a 3 mm / sz 3 needle on the right front piece, moss stitch these. Pick up 19 (19) 21 (21) st along the front neck, and 21 (23) 25 (25) st along the back neck, 19 (19) 21 (21) along the left front, and knit moss stitch over the saved 5 st = 69 (71) 77 (77) st. Knit moss stitch and make sure that the moss stitches go with the front edge st, knit 1 row, make the last buttonhole above the others; knit 6 rows altogether. Cast off in moss stitch.
Sew side and arm seams.
Sew the arms to the cardigan.
Gently press the seams. Sew the buttons on.

FLOWERS

Crochet a number of flowers in various colors the following way: Cast on 7 ch; place them together as a circle with a slipstitch.
Next row: * 2 ch, 1 dc, 1 sl st; repeat from * another 3 times, cut and fasten the yarn.
Sew them to the cardigan.

Sweater vest

The sweater vest has to be one of the world's greatest garments. It's warm and makes one look dressed up in a matter of seconds, no matter if you're five or fifty.

SIZES
2 (4) 6 (8) 10 years

MEASUREMENTS
Length: 13.5 (14.5) 16 (17.5) 19 inches / 34 (37) 40 (44) 48 cm
Periphery: 20.5 (24.5) 26 (29) 32.5 inches / 58 (62) 66 (74) 82 cm

MATERIALS
Yarn: 2 (2) 3 (3) 4 x 50 g / 1.7 oz. of a medium-thick tweed yarn (about 175 st / 50g) and a small amount of contrast color for the stripes
Needles: 3.5 mm / sz 4 mm and 4 mm / sz 6, stitch holder

GAUGE
22 st and 30 rows = 4x4 inch / 10x10 cm double moss stitch on 4 mm / sz 6 needle

BACK PIECE
Cast on 63 (69) 73 (81) 91 st of red yarn on 3.5 mm / sz 4 mm needle. Rib knit, k1, p1, and make stripes the following way: 3 rows red, 2 rows brown, 2 rows red, 2 rows brown, 3 rows red = 12 rows rib knit. Switch to 4 mm / sz 6 needle and double moss stitch:
Row 1: k1, p1; repeat the rest of the row.
Row 3: p1, k1; repeat the rest of the row.
Row 2 and 4: Knit garter stitch on garter stitch and purl stitch on purl stitch. Continue in double moss stitch until the work measures 8.5 (9) 10 (10.5) 11.5 inches / 21 (23) 25 (27) 29 cm.

ARMHOLES
Cast on 3 st on each side. Decrease 1 st on each side on every row 3 times, then on every other row until you are left with 49 (55) 57 (63) 65 st. Continue without decreasing until the back piece measures 13.5 (14.5) 16 (17.5) 19 inches / 34 (37) 40 (44) 48 cm. Cast off.

FRONT PIECE
Cast on and knit like the back piece, up until the last decrease for the armhole.

V-NECK
Knit 24 (27) 28 (31) 32 st, turn and save the remaining st on a stitch holder or spare needle for now. Knit each side separately.
First decrease 1 st for the V-neck on every row 2 times, then on every other row until you are left with 13 (14) 16 (18) 20 st. Continue until the front measures the same as the back up by the shoulder, cast off.
Go back to the saved st, save the middle st on a safety pin, knit like the first side but mirrored.

TIPS & TRICKS
■ If you prefer a deeper V-neck you can start earlier, for instance, after two decreases for the armhole. In that case, pick up a few more stitches along the V-neck so that the rib knit doesn't seem tight.

Row 1 (wrong side): p1, (k1, p1), repeat from the middle stitch, purl knit the middle st, rib knit the rest of the row.

Row 2: k1 (p1, k1) repeat up until 2 st before the middle st, s1, k1, psso, garter knit the middle st, k2 tog, rib knit the rest of the row.

Row 3: Rib knit up until 2 st before the middle st, p2 tog, purl knit the middle st, p2 tog through the backstitch loop, rib knit the rest of the row.

Continue decreasing 1 st on each side of the middle st the same way you did for row 2 and 3; knit 6 rows altogether, cast off in rib knit and decrease the same way as before. Sew the other shoulder together and the short side of the neckline.

ARMHOLE EDGES

Pick up about 61 (67) 73 (79) 87 st with a 3.5 mm / sz 4 mm needle around the armhole, rib knit 6 rows, k1, p1, and make stripes the same way you did around the neck. Sew the side and arm seams together. Gently press down on the seams.

COMPLETION

Clamp the pieces out in accordance with the measurements and cover with a damp cloth; let it dry. Sew the right shoulder together. Work from the straight side, pick up st of red yarn with a 3.5 mm / sz 4 mm needle the following way: Pick up 23 (25) 27 (29) 31 st along the left side of the front neck, move the saved st onto the needle, pick up 23 (25) 27 (29) 31 st along the front right side and lastly, 25 (25) 25 (27) 31 st along the back neck. Rib knit, k1, p1, knit 2 rows with the red yarn, 2 rows with brown and 2 rows with red the following way:

Bolero

The bolero is best suited for parties or for reasonably gentle playing—the material is strong, but the sweater is not the easiest to wash. On the other hand, it is irresistible with its ruffled edges.

SIZES
2 (4) 6 (8) years

MEASUREMENTS
Length: 9.5 (10) 12 (13.5) inches / 24 (26) 30 (34) cm
Periphery: 23 (25) 27.5 (15) inches / 58 (64) 70 (76) cm
Arm length: 9.5 (10.5) 12 (13) inches / 24 (27) 30 (33) cm

MATERIALS
Yarn: 4 (5) 6 (7) x 50 g / 1.7 oz. of a thick alpaca/silk blend yarn (about 115 st / 50 g / 1.7 oz.) 1 ball of a thin mohair/silk blend yarn (about 210 st / 50 g / 1.7 oz.)
Needles: 3.5 mm / sz 4 mm, circular needle 3.5 mm / sz 4 mm, 31.5 inch / 80 cm long

GAUGE
26 st and 34 rows = 4x4 inch / 10x10 cm stockinet stitch with 3.5 mm / sz 4 mm needle

BACK PIECE
Cast on 71 (79) 87 (95) st on a 3.5 mm / sz 4 mm needle, knit stockinet stitch, increase 1 st on each side on the 4th row and then on the 10th row = 75 (83) 91 (99) st. Continue without increasing until the work measures 4.5 (5) 5.5 (6.5) inches / 11 (12) 14 (16) cm.

ARMHOLES
Cast off 4,3 st in each side on every other row = 61 (69) 77 (85) st. Decrease 1 st on each side on each row 1 (4) 5 (6) times, then on every other row until you are left with 57 (61) 65 (69) st. Continue without decreasing until the armhole measures 5 (5) 6 (7) inches / 12 (13) 15 (17) cm. Cast off the middle 21 (21) 23 (23) st for the neck and knit each side separately. Save the other st on the needle.
Cast off 3,4 against the neck on every other row. Cast off 13 (15) 16 (18) st for the shoulder. Go back to

the saved st and finish the same way but mirrored.

LEFT FRONT PIECE
Cast on 24 (28) 31 (34) st on 3.5 mm / sz 4 mm needle, knit stockinet stitch. Knit 2 rows; start casting on for the rounded front edge the following way:
Cast on 4,3,2 (4,3,2,2) 4,3,3,2 (4,4,3,2) at the front edge on every other row, also increase 1 st on the left side on the 4th row and later on the 10th row once = 35 (41) 45 (49) st. Continue without increasing until the front measures the same as the back up by the armhole.

ARMHOLE
Cast off 4,3 st on the left side on every other row = 28 (34) 38 (42) st. Decrease for the armhole the same way you did for the back piece. Also start decreasing for the V-neck at the same time as the first decrease for the armhole.

COMPLETION
Clamp the pieces out in accordance with the measurements. Cover with a damp cloth and let dry.
Sew the shoulders together. Sew the sides together.

RUFFLED EDGE
Work from the straight side, start at one side, pick up st around the outer edge of the bolero with the circular needle and the mohair yarn.
Pick up st the following way:
Along the bottom edge and back neck you pick up 1 st in every st. Along the row's short sides you pick up 2 st over 3 rows (in other words pick up 2 rows and then skip the 3rd and so on). Knit round in stockinet stitch. Increase 1 st in each st on the next row. Knit 3 rows. Cast off.
Make the same ruffled edges on the arms, but knit the rows back and forth.
Sew the arms together and sew them to the cardigan. Gently press down on the seams.

Decrease 1 st for the neck on every 3rd row until you are left with 13 (15) 16 (18) st, cast off when the front measures the same as the back up by the shoulder.

RIGHT FRONT PIECE
Cast on and knit like the left but mirrored.

ARMS
Cast on 43 (46) 51 (55) st on a 3.5 mm / sz 4 mm needle, knit stockinet stitch, also increase 1 st on each side on every 8th row until you have 63 (69) 75 (81) st, continue without increasing until the arm measures 9.5 (10.5) 12 (13) inches / 24 (27) 30 (33) cm.

ARM CAP
Cast off 4,3 st on each side = 49 (55) 61 (67) st. Continue decreasing 1 st on each side on every row 3 times. Cast off 5,4 st on each side = 25 (31) 37 (43). Cast off.

Cool hooded jacket

This hooded jacket may be knitted in many varieties. Here we have chosen to knit the front edge in a contrast color—a small detail that makes the entire jacket more fun. The zipper can also be substituted for buttons.

SIZES
4 (6) 8 (10) years

MATERIALS
Yarn: 5 (6) 7 (8) x 50 g / 1.7 oz. of a thin wool/cotton yarn (about 115 st / 50g) and one ball of the same material (in optional contrasting color) for the front edge
Needles: 4 mm / sz 6
Other: 5–7 buttons or zipper

GAUGE
23 st and 31 rows = 4x4 inch / 10x10 cm moss stitch on 4 mm / sz 6 needle

MOSS STITCH
Moss stitch (= rib knit that is shifted, garter stitch on purl stitch and purl stitch on garter knit):
Row 1: * k1, p1; repeat from * the rest of the row.
Row 2: * p1, k1; repeat from * the rest of the row.

BACK PIECE
Cast on 72 (80) 84 (92) st and knit moss stitch. Knit until the back piece measures 10.5 (12) 12.5 (13.5) inches / 27 (30) 32 (34) cm. Now decrease for the armhole on each side 3,2,1,1 st to 58 (66) 70 (78) st. When the armhole measures 6 (6.5) 7 (7) inches / 15 (16) 17 (18) cm from the first cast off, cast off the middle 16 (18) 18 (20) st and knit each side separately. Cast off for the shoulder and the neck at the same time. For the shoulder cast off 5 (6) 7 (8) st 2 times; for the neck first cast off 3 st and then 2 st. Cast off the remaining 6 (7) 7 (8) st. Knit the other shoulder the same way.

LEFT FRONT PIECE
Cast on 38 (42) 45 (48) st and moss stitch. Knit until the front piece reaches the cast off for the arm on the back piece. Now decrease 3,2,1,1 st for the armhole at the beginning of the row to 31 (35) 38 (41) st. When the armhole is 3.5 (4) 4 (4.5) inches / 9 (10) 10 (11) cm shorter than the back piece cast off for the neck and shoulder then cast off for the neck from the wrong side with 4,4,3,2,1,1 (5,4,3,2,1,1,1) 5,4,3,2,1,1,1 (5,4,3,2,1,1,1) so that you are left with 16 (19) 21 (24) st. Cast off for the shoulder the same way you did for the back piece.

RIGHT FRONT PIECE

Knit the same way you did for the left piece but mirrored.

ARMS

Cast on 44 (48) 52 (56) st and knit moss stitch. Increase 1 st on each side after 2.5 inch / 6 cm and then on every 8th row until there are 58 (64) 70 (76) st on the needle. When the arm measures 30 (33) 36 (39) st, cast off on each side 3,2,1,1. Knit 1.5 inch / 3 cm. Cast off 2,3,4, st, cast off the remaining st.

FRONT EDGES

Pick up 1 st out of each row (skip every 10th row) from the bottom to the neckline with the contrast color. Garter knit the front edges. The front edges are knitted the same way regardless of whether you are using buttons or a zipper. They are both 3 rows.
If you want buttons to distinguish between boy-and girl-buttoning, knit buttonholes on the right front edge for girls and the left front edge for boys. Cast off for buttonholes 1 or 2 st on the 3rd row on the front edge, cast on the equal number of st on the next row. Knit another 2 rows, cast off.

COMPLETION

Press all of the pieces. Sew the shoulder seams. Wait to sew the arms on until the hood is knitted to avoid making the knitting too heavy to hold.

HOOD

Pick up stitches for the hood along the front of the neckline (keep on the inside of the knitted front edge). Pick up about 79 (85) 91 (97) st from the straight side. If you do not pick this exact number, adjust on the first row. Place a marker on each side of the middle 21 (23) 25 (27) stitches of the back piece and increase outside of these marks with 1 st on each side on every 4th row until there are 87 (95) 103 (111) st on the needle. When the hood is 10.5 (11) 11.5 (12) inches / 21 (22) 23 (24) cm at the middle of the back, cast off the middle 24 (26) 28 (30) st. Knit each side separately. When the sides of the hood reach the middle of the cast-off middle stitches (fold in and keep track, it is easy to knit too far), knit 1 more row. Cast off. Sew the knitted edges of the side pieces against the cast off in the middle straight against straight, then sew the cast off edges of the side pieces against each other straight against straight.

TIPS & TRICKS

■ If you prefer a more traditional jacket you can knit it in stockinet stitch. In that case knit 2 inch / 5 cm moss stitch as a bottom edge on all the pieces, and knit the rest in stockinet stitch. The jacket will then be somewhat smaller.
■ You are free to experiment with colors here. The jacket can be a plain color, striped, have a hood, have a front edge in contrasting colors—whatever you can think of is possible.
■ The hood can also be left out; in that case you'll need a small collar. See the pattern on p. 35 for inspiration. Preferably, it is knitted with the same technique as the edges, such as the moss stitch.

Chanel cardigan

This simple cardigan suddenly receives a unique touch when ribbon is sewn on. The ribbons chosen are a nod to Chanel; if you choose another ribbon the look will be completely different. The dress is knitted in the same yarn (see p. 86), and if you decorate the dress with the same ribbon you get a nice complete look.

SIZES
2 (4) 6 (8) years

MEASUREMENTS
Length: 13.5 (15) 16.5 (18) inches / 34 (38) 42 (46) cm
Periphery: 25 (26.5) 28.5 (31) inches / 64 (68) 72 (78) cm
Arm length: 9.5 (11) 12.5 (15) inches / 24 (28) 32 (38) cm

MATERIALS
Yarn: 4 (5) 6 (7) x 50 g / 1.7 oz. of a medium-thick yarn in extra fine merino wool (about 115 st / 50g)
Needles: 4 mm / sz 6
Other: about 5 (5) 6.5 (6.5) feet / 1.5 (1.5) 2 (2) meters ribbon to decorate

GAUGE
22 st and 30 rows = 4x4 inch / 10x10 cm stockinet stitch on 4 mm / sz 6 needle

BACK PIECE
Cast on 71 (75) 79 (85) st on 4 mm needle, garter knit 3 rows. Move onto stockinet stitch and knit until the work measures 7.5 (9) 10 (11.5) inches / 19 (22) 26 (29) cm.

ARMHOLES
Cast off 4 st on each side. Decrease 1 st on every other row 3 times, then on every other row until you are left with 53 (57) 61 (67) st. Continue without decreasing until the work measures 13 (14.5) 16.5 (18) inches / 33 (37) 42 (45) cm. Cast off the middle 15 (15) 17 (19) for the neck and knit each side separately. Save the other on the needle.
Cast off 4 st against the neck at the beginning of the next row. Cast off 5,5,5 (5,6,6) 6,6,6 (6,7,7) st on every other row for the shoulder.

Go back to the saved stitches and finish like before but mirrored.

LEFT FRONT PIECE

Cast on 36 (38) 40 (43) st on 4 mm / sz 6 needle and garter knit 3 rows. Move on to stockinet stitch, but continue to knit the outer 3 st with garter stitch for the front edge. Knit until the front measures the same as the back up by the cast off for the armhole; finish from the wrong side.

ARMHOLES

Cast off 4 st for the armhole. Decrease 1 st on each row 3 times, then on every other row until you are left with 26 (28) 32 (35) st.
Continue in stockinet and moss stitch until the front piece measures 2 (2) 2.5 (3) inches / 5 (5) 6 (7) cm shorter than the back measures from the first cast off for the shoulder.

NECK

Cast off 4,3 st for the neck on every other row, decrease 1 st for the neck on every other row until you are left with 15 (17) 18 (20) st. Continue until the front measures the same as the back up by the shoulder, cast off for the shoulder the same way you did for the back.

RIGHT FRONT PIECE

Cast on and knit like the left front piece except mirrored.

ARMS

Cast on 41 (43) 45 (47) st on 4 mm / sz 6 needle, garter knit 3 rows, move on to stockinet stitch and increase 1 st on each side (keep on the inside of the outer 2 st) on the 3rd and later on every 6th (6th) 8th (8th) row until you have 55 (57) 59 (61) st on the needle. Continue without increasing until the arm measures 9.5 (11) 12.5 (14.5) inches / 24 (28) 32 (36) cm.

ARM CAP

Cast off 4 st on each side. Decrease 1 st on each side on every row, 3 times, then on every other row 6 (6) 2 (2) times = 29 (31) 41 (43) st. On the two largest sizes you now decrease on every 4th row until there are 35 (37) st left. Now decrease 1 st on each side until there are 21 (21) 23 (23) st left. Cast off all stitches.

COMPLETION

Clamp the pieces out after the measurements, cover with a damp cloth and let it dry.
Sew the shoulders together.

NECKLINE

Pick up 63 (67) 71 (73) st with a 4 mm / sz 6 needle from the straight side around the neck, garter knit 3 rows, cast off. Sew the sides together. Start by the one side and sew the ribbon to the cardigan's edges and neck, fold the ribbon around the corners.
Fasten with small stitches.
Repeat at the bottom arm edges.
Sew the arms onto the cardigan.
Gently press down on the seams.

Knitted dress

A quicker-to-knit dress is hard, if not impossible, to find; the only thing that may take some time here is the adding of a ribbon or embroidered flowers. The dress may be used in summer without the cardigan, and during wintertime with the cardigan (see p. 83).

SIZES
2 (4) 6 (8) years

MEASUREMENTS
Length: 19 (20.5) 23 (24.5) inches / 48 (52) 58 (62) cm
Periphery (around the chest): 22 (23.5) 26 (27.5) inches / 56 (60) 66 (70) cm

MATERIALS
Yarn: 5 (6) 7 (8) x 50 g / 1.7 oz. of a medium-thick wool/cotton yarn (about 115 st / 50g)
Needles: 3.5 mm / sz 4 mm and 4 mm / sz 6

GAUGE
24 st and 32 rows = 4x4 inch / 10x10 cm stockinet stitch on 3 mm / sz 3 needle

BACK PIECE
Cast on 100 (108) 116 (124) st on 3.5 mm / sz 4 mm needle, garter knit for 1 inch / 2 cm, change to 4 mm / sz 6 needle and stockinet stitch.
Knit 4 rows, start the decreases in the sides the following way:
Next row (garter): k3, sl1, k1, psso, knit up until the last 5 st, k2 tog, k3.
Continue decreasing on every 6th row until you are left with 66 (72) 78 (84) st. Continue without decreasing until the work measures 13.5 (15) 16.5 (18) inches / 34 (38) 42 (46) cm.

ARMHOLES
Cast off 7 (8) 8 (9) st on each side. Now decrease on the inside of the outer st like before and decrease 1 st on each side on every row 3 times, then on every other row until there are 42 (46) 50 (54) st left. Continue without decreasing until the armhole measures 5 (5.5) 6 (6.5) inches / 13 (14) 15 (16) cm.

NECK AND SHOULDERS
Cast off the middle 20 (22) 24 (26) st for the neck and knit each side separately. Cast off 2 st against the neck at the beginning of the next row, then decrease 1 st on every other row until there are 8 (9) 10 (11) st for the shoulder. Knit until the work measures 20 (22) 24 (26) inches / 51 (55) 61 (66) cm, cast off the last st. Return to the saved st and finish like you did for the first side except mirrored.

FRONT PIECE
Cast on and knit like the back piece until the armhole measures 2 (2.5) 3 (3) inches / 5 (6) 7 (8) cm.

NECK
Cast off the middle 12 (14) 16 (18) st for the neck and knit each side separately. Cast off another 2 st against the neck. Then decrease 1 st for the neck on every row 2 times, then on

TIPS & TRICKS
■ The dress will change its character completely if (just like the cardigan) it is decorated with ribbons. An Eastern-inspired ribbon may give one impression, while a pink ribbon with flowers will say something completely different.

every other row until there are 8 (9) 10 (11) st left. Continue knitting until the front measures the same as the back up by the shoulder, cast off. Return to the saved st and finish like the first side except mirrored.

COMPLETION
Clamp the parts out after the measurements, cover with a damp cloth and let it dry.
Sew the right shoulder together.

NECKLINE
Pick up about 100 (106) 112 (120) st from the straight side evenly distributed around the neck with a 3.5 mm / sz 4 mm needle. Garter kit 5 rows, cast off with garter stitches. Sew the other shoulder together and the short side of the neckline.

ARMHOLE EDGES
Pick up about 84 (88) 92 (94) st evenly distributed around the armhole from the straight side with a 3.2 mm needle. Garter knit 5 rows, cast off with garter stitches. Sew the sides together. Gently press down on the seams.

Roughly - knitted polo sweater

When the autumn sets in it will be especially nice to have a thick sweater to crawl into. A mild earth color makes the sweater very usable; it is just as pretty with jeans as it is with dress pants.

SIZES
2 (4) 6 (8) 10 years

MEASUREMENTS
Length: 14 (16) 17.5 (20) 22 inches / 36 (40) 44 (50) 56 cm
Periphery: 26 (29) 31 (33) 35.5 inches / 66 (74) 78 (84) 90 cm
Arm length: 9.5 (11) 12.5 (15) 16.5 inches / 24 (28) 32 (38) 42 cm

MATERIALS
Yarn: 5 (6) 7 (7) 9x50 g / 1.7 oz. of a thick wool yarn (about 88 st /50g)
Needles: 5 mm / sz 8 and 6 mm / sz 10

GAUGE
16 st and 22 rows = 4x4 inch / 10x10 cm stockinet stitch on 5 mm / sz 8 needle

BACK PIECE
Cast on 57 (61) 65 (69) 73 st on 5 mm / sz 8 needle. Rib knit, k1, p1, for 2 (2) 2.5 (2.5) 2.5 inches / 5 (5) 6 (6) 6 cm. Switch to 6 mm / sz 10 needle and increase 6 st evenly over the first row = 63 (67) 71 (75) 71 st. Knit until the work measures 8 (9.5) 11 (12.5) 14 inches / 20 (24) 28 (32) 36 cm.

ARMHOLES
Cast off 5 (6) 6 (7) 7 st on each side, then decrease 1 st on each side on every other row 3 times = 47 (49) 53 (55) st. Continue until the work measures 14 (15.5) 17 (19.5) 21.7 inches / 35 (39) 43 (49) 55 cm.

SHOULDERS AND NECK
Cast off the middle 17 (19) 21 (23) 23 st for the neck and knit each side separately. Save the other st on the needle. Cast off 3 st for the neck at the beginning of the next row. Cast off the remaining 12 (12) 13 (13) 15 st for the shoulder. Return to the saved st and finish like the first side but mirrored.

FRONT PIECE
Cast on and knit like the back until the work measures 2.5 (3) 3 (3.5) 4 inches / 6 (7) 8 (9) 10 cm shorter than the back when measured from the shoulder.

NECK
Cast off the middle 9 (11) 13 (15) 17 st for the neck and knit each side separately. Save the other st on the needle. Cast off in two turns on every other row 3,2 st. Now decrease 1 st against the neck until there are 12 (12) 13 (13) 15 st left, continue knitting these until the front measures the same as the back up by the shoulder, cast off. Return to the saved st and finish like the first side except mirrored.

ARMS
Cast on 31 (31) 33 (33) 35 st on 5 mm / sz 8 needle, rib knit, k1, p1, for 2 inches / 5 cm. Switch to 6 mm / sz 10 needle and stockinet stitch; increase 1 st on each side on the next row and later on every 4th row

until there are 49 (55) 59 (63) 65 st. Continue without increasing until the arm measures 9.5 (11) 12.5 (15) 16.5 inches / 24 (28) 32 (38) 42 cm.

ARM CAP

Cast off 5 (6) 6 (7) 7 st on each side. Decrease 1 st on each side of every other row 3 times.
Cast off the remaining 33 (37) 41 (43) 45 st.

COMPLETION

Clamp all of the pieces out. Cover with a damp cloth and let this dry. Sew the right shoulder together.

POLO COLLAR

Pick up about 65 (69) 73 (79) 81 st from the straight side evenly distributed around the neck with a 6 mm / sz 10 needle. Rib knit, k1, p1, for 4 (5) 5 (5.5) 5.5 inches / 10 (12) 12 (14) 14 cm (or the preferred length), cast off in rib knit.
Sew the left shoulder together and the short side of the collar. Turn the seam inside out after about half the seam, since the collar will be folded outwards.
Sew the arms to the sweater. Sew the side and arm seams. Gently press down on the seams.

Tweed cardigan

It doesn't get much easier than this. This quick cardigan in a rough yarn is knitted in garter knit only; there isn't even a complicated collar.

SIZES
3–4 (5) 6–8 (8–10) years

MATERIALS
Yarn: 4 (5) 6 (7) x 50 g / 1.7 oz. / 1.7 oz. yarn of a rough tweed or wool (about 87 st /50 g / 1.7 oz. / 1.7 oz.)
Needles: size 5
Other: 6–7 buttons

GAUGE
16 st and 23 rows = 4x4 inch / 10x10 cm garter knit with 5 mm / sz 8 needle

BACK PIECE
Cast on 56 (58) 60 (64) st and garter knit 13.5 (15) 16 (16.5) inches / 34 (38) 40 (42) cm. Cast off the middle 18 (20) 22 (24) st for the neck, and knit each side separately. Each side should have 19 (19) 19 (20) st. Cast off 3 st for the neck. Cast off the remaining 16 (16) 16 (17) st for the shoulder.

LEFT FRONT PIECE
Cast on 32 (33) 34 (36) st and knit until the front piece measures 2 cm / 1 inchshorter than the decrease for the neck on the back piece. Cast off for the neck from the wrong side on every other row with 5,4,3,2,1,1 (5,4,3,2,2,1) 5,4,3,3,2,1 (5,4,43,2,1) st. Cast off the remaining 16 (16) 16 (17) st for the shoulder.

RIGHT FRONT PIECE
(including buttonholes)
This piece is knitted like the left front piece but in the opposite direction. Make a buttonhole from the straight side as close as you want the buttons to be (we have made buttonholes on every 8th row). Make the holes by starting from the straight side, k3, 1 YO, k2 tog; garter knit the rest of the row.

ARMS
If you prefer not to fold the edges of the sleeves, decrease the total length about 1.5 inches / 4 cm. Cast on 28 (30) 32 (34) st and garter knit 3 inches / 8 cm. Follow by increasing 1 st on each side on every 4th row until there are 62 (66) 74 (78) st on the needle.
Continue knitting until the arm measures 12.5 (14) 16 (17.5) inches / 32 (36) 40 (44) cm. Cast off.

TIPS & TRICKS

■ This cardigan is especially pretty if it is decorated with some embroidery (perhaps along the edges of the arms).

■ If you wish to make a durable party cardigan you can add a thin glitter yarn and knit with two yarns (either the whole garment or in stripes). Black base yarn and a glittery yarn in gold or silver look fantastic.

COMPLETION

Sew the shoulder seams. Sew the arms to the cardigan so that the middle of the arm is situated at the middle of the shoulder seam. Sew side and arm seams. If you wish you can turn the work and sew the bottom edge of the arm wrong side against the wrong side, this way the arm will be folded inwards when you fold the sleeves.

Poncho

This durable poncho ended up in this color combination purely by chance; we had some blue yarn leftover—good example of making use of what you have and ending up with a great result. The poncho, of course, may also be knitted in just one color.

SIZES
2 (4) 6 (8) 10 years

MEASUREMENTS
Length, measured to the tip excluding the fringe: 18.5 (20) 21 (11) 23 inches / 47 (50) 53 (56) 59 cm
Periphery on top: 29 (31) 32.5 (36) 38 inches / 74 (78) 82 (92) 96 cm
Periphery bottom: 44.5 (49) 53 (57.5) 62 inches / 113 (124) 135 (146) 157 cm

MATERIALS
Yarn: 7 (8) 9 (10) 11 x 50 g / 1.7 oz. / 1.7 oz. and 50 g / 1.7 oz. / 1.7 oz. in a contrast color of a thick wool yarn (about 87 st / 50g)
Needles: circular needles 4.5 mm (length 23.5 inches / 60 cm) and 5 mm / sz 8 (length 23.5 inches / 60 cm and 31.5 inches / 80 cm)

GAUGE
16 st and 20 rows = 4x4 inch / 10x10 cm stockinet stitch on 5 mm / sz 8 needle

STRIPE PATTERN
After the moss stitch, start knitting the stripes:
2 rows, base color, 3 rows in contrast color
1 row base color, 2 rows contrast color
1 row base color, 1 row contrast color
Continue with the base color. Make decreases in accordance with the pattern.

PONCHO (knitted in one piece)
Cast on 184 (194) 214 (234) 244 st on a circular 5 mm needle, length 31.5 inches / 80 cm.
Knit moss stitch for 6 (8) 8 (10) 10 rows, move on to stockinet stitch. Place a yarn mark on the middle front and the middle back. Now start the decreases.
Decrease the following way: * knit up until the last 2 st before the mark, Sl1, k1, psso, move over the mark, k2 tog, knit up until the next mark; repeat from *.
Decrease like this on every 3rd row until you have 122 (134) 146 (158) 170 st left. (NOTE: Switch to the shorter circular needle when the st are not long enough.)

DECREASE FOR THE SHOULDERS
Place a marker in the middle of the two other markers so that you now have 4 markers. Decrease like you did before on each side of the four markers and now on every other row until there are 66 (70) 74 (78) 82 st. Switch to the circular needle 4.5 mm and rib knit, k1, p1, for 1 inch / 2 cm.

ROW OF EYELET HOLES
Next row: Continue in rib knit like before, * k3, k2 tog, 1 YO; repeat from * the rest of the row.
Continue in rib knit until the neckline measures 2 (2) 2.5 (3) 3 inches / 5 (5) 6 (7) 8 cm.
Cast off in rib knit.

COMPLETION

Clamp the poncho out, place
a damp cloth on top and let it
dry. Make fringes (see p. 106)
and tie them along the bottom
edge.
The ties in the picture are
16–23.5 inch- / 40–60 cm-long
regular braids with triple yarn.
Thread in the holes by the neck.

Woolen socks

Woolen socks can be knitted in a number of colors other than the classic gray and white. Here we have chosen to make the heel plain and the shaft striped; however, variation possibilities are endless.

SIZES
2 (4) 6 (8) 10 years

MEASUREMENTS
Foot length: 6 (7) 7.5 (8.5) 9 inches / 15 (17) 19 (21) 23 cm

MATERIALS
Yarn: 1 (2) 2 (2) 2 x50 g / 1.7 oz. / 1.7 oz. of a medium-thick wool yarn (about 115 st / 50 g / 1.7 oz. / 1.7 oz.)
Needles: double-pointed needles 4 mm / sz 6

GAUGE
11st and 16 rows = 1.5x1.5 inch / 4x4cm stockinet stitch on 4 mm / sz 6 needle

The sock needles are named the following way: needle no. 1 and 4 have the sock's backside (heel) and needle no.2 and 3 the upper part.

Cast on. 36 (36) 40 (44) 48 st on one of the needles. Distribute the st over the 4 needles, rib knit in the round, k2, p2, for 5 (5) 5.5 (6.5) 6.5 inches / 12 (12) 14 (16) 16 cm. Start the heel with needle 1 and 4, in other words over 18 (18) 20 (22) 24 st. Stockinet stitch back and forth on the rows for 3.5 mm / sz 4 (1.5) 1.7 (1.9)

(2) inches / (3.5) 4 (4.5) 5 cm. Knit the heel together the following way: Work from the straight side and knit 10 (10) 11 (12) 13 garter stitches, k2 tog, k1, turn, p4, p2 tog, p1, turn; k5, k2 tog, k1, turn, k5, k1 tog, k1, turn; knit one more st before all of the increases for all the st are knitted together on each side. Knit the rest of the heel the follow-ing way: Pick up 5 (5) 6 (7) 8 st on each side of the heel, knit in the round over all the 4 needles, also

knit 2 st together on each side of the st you picked up on every other row. Knit together by knitting 2 st together at the end of needle 1 and Sl1, k1, psso at the beginning of needle 4. Decrease until you are left with 32 (34) 36 (40) 44 st. (NOTE: The increases are happening with the heel's st.)
Knit in the round until the foot measures 5 (5) 5.5 (6) 6.5 inches / 12 (13) 14 (15) 16 cm (or the pre-ferred length), measured from the outer edge of the heel.
Decrease for the toe the following way: k2 tog at the end of needle 1 and needle 3; keep within the last outer st, in other words, knit until there are 3 st left on the needle, k2 tog, k1. On needle 2 and needle 4 Sl1, k1, psso after the first st, in other words, k1, Sl1, k1, psso. Do these decreases on every other row 3 (3) 3 (4) 4 times, and then on every row until there are 8 st left. Cut the yarn and pull through the st. Fasten carefully.

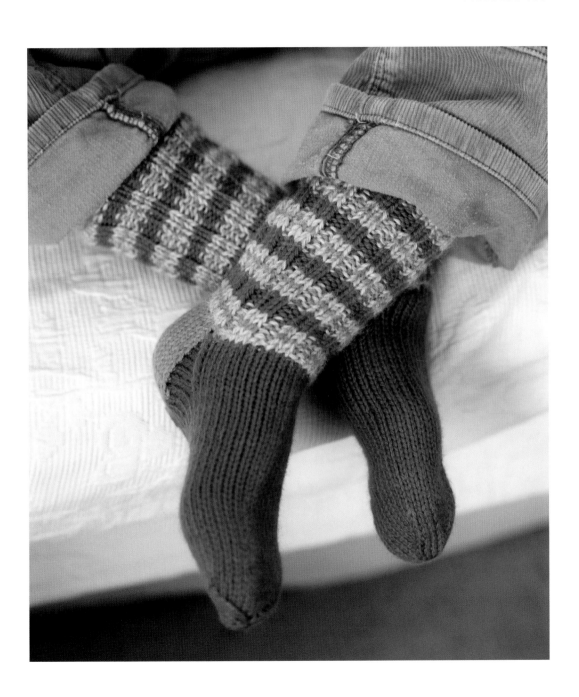

Rib-knit beanie

Beanies have once more gained popularity after years of hiding in the dresser. They are quick to knit and therefore great to knit in multiple colors.

SIZE
One size fits all

MATERIALS
Yarn: 50 g / 1.7 oz. / 1.7 oz. of a thick wool yarn (about 87 st /50 g / 1.7 oz. / 1.7 oz.)
Needles: 4 mm / sz 6 and 5 mm / sz 8

GAUGE
18 st and 22 rows = 4x4 inch / 10x10 cm rib knit on 5 mm / sz 8 needle

Cast on 86 st on 4 mm / sz 6 needle, start and finish every row with a garter stitch as an edge stitch (that is outside of the pattern). Rib knit 8 rows, k1, p1. Switch to 5 mm / sz 8 needle and rib knit, k3, p3, continue until the work measures 6.5 inches / 16 cm or the wanted height.

DECREASE FOR THE TOP
Row 1 (garter): (k3, p3 tog); repeat through the whole row = 58 st.
Row 2: (k1, p3); repeat through the whole row.
Row 3: (k3, p1); repeat through the whole row.
Row 4: Same as row 2.
Next row: (k3 tog, p1); repeat through the whole row = 30 st.
Next row: (k1, p1); repeat through the whole row.
Next row: k2 tog, the whole row. Cut the yarn (save a piece for sewing the beanie together), thread through st. Pull and fasten. Sew the beanie together.

Striped beanie

Stripes are a great way to make a simple garment look more detailed—and the colors may be endlessly varied. If you are knitting a regular, simple beanie like this, you can also give it a personal touch by adding one or more tassels in your color of choice.

SIZES
2–4 (6–8) 10–12 years

MATERIALS
Yarn: 1 ball/ 50 g / 1.7 oz. / 1.7 oz. for each color of a medium-thick merino wool yarn (about 115 st / 50g) Our beanie is knitted in two color combinations: the first in orange, turquoise, lime green, and purple; the other in gray, white, black, and light blue.
Needles: 3.5 mm / sz 4 mm (if you want a rib-knit edge) and 4 mm / sz 6

GAUGE
22 st and 30 rows = 4x4 inch / 10x10 cm stockinet stitch on 4 mm / sz 6 needle

MODEL WITH RIB KNIT EDGE
Cast on 91 (95) 101 st of the turquoise or gray yarn on 3.5 mm / sz 4 mm needle, rib knit, k1, p1 for 2 cm /1 inch , increase 1 st at the end of the last row = 92 (96) 102 st.

MODEL WITH ROLL-UP EDGE
Cast on 92 (96) 102 st with the turquoise or gray yarn on 4 mm / sz 6 needle, knit 6 rows stockinet stitch.

BOTH MODELS
Knit stockinet stitch and stripes which are, alternately, 2 and 4 rows wide in the following order: Orange, purple, lime-green, turquoise, or white, black, light blue, gray. Continue until the work measures 5 (5) 6 inches / 12 (13) 15 cm, measured after the rib knit/ roll-up edge (or wanted height). On the middle size you decrease 4 st evenly distributed on the 4th row = 92 (92) 102.

DECREASE FOR THE TOP
Row 1: k2, k [7(7)8, k2 tog], repeat until the last st which you garter stitch.
Row 2: Purl stitch.
Row 3: k 1 (2) 1, * k [6(6) 7, k2 tog, repeat until the last st, which you garter stitch.
Continue decreasing on every other row with 1 st less between the knitting decreases until there are 12 st left.
Cut the yarn and pull through the st. Sew the beanie together in the back and fasten.

TIPS & TRICKS

■ You can make one or more yarn pompoms (see p. 107) or decorate with a flower.

A flower knitted in two parts and sewn together:

FLOWER 1

Cast on 49 st.
Row 1: k1, * cast off 5 st, k1, repeat from * the rest of the row = 9 st.
Row 2: Knit 1 st in the front and back stitch loop on every stitch = 18 st.
Row 3: Garter knit.
Row 4: Purl knit.
Row 4: Purl knit.
Row 5: Garter knit.
Row 6: Purl 2 st together; repeat the rest of the row = 9 st.
Cut the yarn and thread it through the st, pull and fasten, sew the short ends together.

FLOWER 2

Cast on 31 st.
Row 1: k1, * cast off 5 st, k1; repeat from * the rest of the row = 6st.
Row 2: Knit 2 garter stitches in the front and backstitch loop of every stitch = 12 m.
Row 3: Garter knit.
Row 4: p2 tog, repeat through the entire row = 6 st.
Cut the yarn and thread it through st, pull and fasten, sew the short ends together.

Sew the flowers together and fasten them on the beanie.

Mittens

Thick wool mittens are unbeatable in winter. Try them solid, patterned, or with some sort of embroidery.

SIZES
2–4 (6–8) 10–12 years

MEASUREMENTS
Length measured from the wrist: 5 (5) 3 inches / 12 (13) 16 cm
Periphery: 7 (8) 9 inches / 14 (16) 18 cm

MATERIALS
Yarn: 1 (1) 2x50 g / 1.7 oz. / 1.7 oz. of a thick wool yarn (about 115 st / 50 g)
Needles: Double-pointed needles 4 mm / sz 6

GAUGE
11 st and 15 rows = 1.5x1.5 inch / 4x4cm stockinet stitch on 4 mm / sz 6 needle

The needles are numbered the following way: Needle numbers 1 and 4 are for the underside of the mitten and numbers 2 and 3 are for the upper side.

LEFT MITT
Cast on 28 (32) 36 st, distribute between the 4 needles; make sure that none of the stitches are twisted, rib knit in the round, k2, p2, for 2 (2) 3 inches / 5 (5) 7 cm (or to the wanted length). Switch to stockinet stitch and knit 4 rows.

THUMB WEDGE
Knit until there are 3 st left on needle no. 1, pick up the thread between the st and the needle and garter knit it twisted, knit 1 stitch, increase 1 st the same way you did the first increase. Continue increasing on every other row 4 (5) 6 times until the thumb wedge has reached the thumb grip. Move the 9 (11) 13 st of the thumb wedge over on a thread. Cast on 1 st and continue until the mitten measures 5 (6) 7 inches / 13 (15) 18 cm or the preferred length.
Knit the mitten together the following way: Continue in stockinet stitch, Sl1, k1, psso at the beginning of needle no. 2 and no. 4 and k2 together at the end of needle no. 1 and no. 3; on the inside of the outer st, do a decrease on every other row 3 times, then on every row until you have 6 st left.
Cut the yarn and pull it through the st, pull and fasten.

THUMB
Pick up the 9 (11) 13 st from the thread, pick up 3 new st from the thumb grip, distribute the st over

three needles. Knit the first and last 2 st together on the first row. Knit until the thumb measures 1.2 (1.5) 1.8 inches / 3 (4) 4.5 cm or the preferred length. Knit 2 and 2 st together, cut the yarn and pull it through st, pull and fasten. Fasten all loose yarn ends.

RIGHT MITT

Knit the same way, but place the thumb wedge before the 2nd st on needle no. 4, in other words, knit 2 st, pick the thread up between the st and garter knit it twisted, knit 1 st, increase 1 st the same way you did the first increase.

Scarf in three varieties

Here we have three scarves made with three knitting techniques: fisherman's rib knit, rib knit, and moss stitch. The fisherman's rib is thick and fluffy, the rib knit tight, and the moss-stitched scarf is easy to shape into a nice tie.

MEASUREMENTS
25.5 (35.5) x about 5.5 (7) inches / 65 (90) x about 14 (18) cm

MATERIALS
Yarn: 1 (2) x 50 g / 1.7 oz. / 1.7 oz. of a thin or medium-thick wool yarn (about 160 st / 50 g / 1.7 oz. / 1.7 oz.)
Needles: 4 mm / sz 6 or 5 mm / sz 8 (for thinner or thicker yarn)

FISHERMAN'S RIB KNIT SCARF
Cast on 26 st on a 4 (5) mm needle, knit the following way:

Beginning row: * 1 YO, lift the next st with the yarn behind the work, k1; repeat from * the whole row.
Row 1: * 1 YO, lift the next st with the yarn behind the work, k2 tog (the lifted and the yarned over from the previous row); repeat from * the rest of the row.
Repeat row 1 until you have the preferred length. Loosely cast off.

RIB KNIT SCARF
Cast on 48 st on 4 (5) mm needle, rib knit, k1, p2, for the wanted length, cast off in rib knit. Our scarf is striped in the colors blue, lime, red, yellow and dark pink.

The stripes are alternately 4 and 3 rows wide.

MOSS STITCH SCARF
Cast on 31 st on 4 (5) mm needle.
Row 1: k1, p1.
Repeat row one until you have the wanted length.
Cast off.

COMPLETION
Fasten all loose ends, and spread the scarf out according to the measurements. Place a damp cloth on top and let this dry. Cut and tie fringe if wanted (see p. 106) along the short ends.

Cool handbag with matching scarf

The handbag and scarf is a great project for the knitting beginner, and a quick knit for the more experienced. You can line the bag as well so that it can carry heavier items such as schoolbooks.

MEASUREMENTS
Bag: about 10 inches / 25 cm wide and 11.5 inches / 29 cm deep
Scarf: 6 inches / 15 cm wide and 39.5 inches / 100 cm long

MATERIALS
Yarn: a thick yarn in cotton/acrylic (about 98 st /50 g / 1.7 oz. / 1.7 oz.) in the colors dark brown (color A) and turquoise (color B)
Bag:
2x50 of color A
1x50 of color B
Scarf:
2x50 of color A
2x50 of color B
Needles: 4.5 mm / sz 7

GAUGE
16 st and 23 row = 4x4 inch / 10x10 cm stockinet stitch on 4.5 mm needle

HANDBAG
Cast on 76 st with color A on 4.5 mm / sz 7 needle.
* Stockinet stitch 13 rows.
Change to color B and garter knit 13 rows. Repeat one from *.
Switch to color A and garter knit until the bag measures 10 inches / 25 cm. Now knit a row with eyelet holes for the tie.
K4, * 1 YO, k2 tog, k9; repeat from *.
Garter knit for 8 rows. Cast off from the wrong side.
Tie: Cast on 150 st with color A. cast off with color B right away.

COMPLETION
Sew the bag together on the bottom and the side. Thread the tie through the eyelet holes and tie or sew it together.

SCARF
Cast on 24 st with color A on 4.5 mm / sz 7 needle. Garter knit 13 rows. Switch to color B and garter knit for 13 rows.
Repeat these two stripes of 13 rows until the scarf measures about 39.5 inches / 100 cm.

TIPS & TRICKS
■ The scarf can be embroide-red; use a turquoise color on the brown stripes and embroi-der large Xs or flowers.
■ The bag and scarf also look great in one single color.
■ If you want a wider strap to carry the bag with the tie only used to close the bag, the strap is knitted the following way: Cast on 6 st on 4.5 mm needles. Garter knit until the strap is the preferred length. Cast off and sew it onto the bag.

Fringe

Fringe may be most common as a
finishing touch on scarves, but it may
also be used on sweaters—for instance
a poncho, and other garments.

1. Cut the yarn in strips that are
double the length of the wanted
fringe plus a little extra for the
knot. Thread a crochet needle
through one of the bottom
stitches.

2. Take hold of the loop of the
fringe and pull it through the
stitch.

3. Pull the fringe's ends through
the loop and pull fast.

Pompoms and embroidery

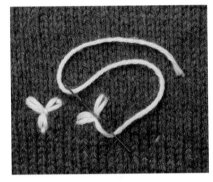

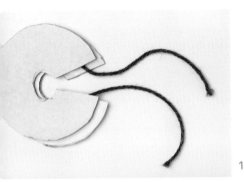

HOW TO MAKE A POMPOM
1. Make two circles out of cardboard, the diameter should be the same as the size of the finished pompom. Cut a hole in the middle and cut a "slice of pie" out as pictured. Place a piece of yarn between the two circles.
2. Wind the yarn around the cardboard circles the preferred amount of times. Wind tightly. Then cut the edges of the yarn between the two cardboard pieces.
3. Pull out and tie the piece of yarn that is lying between the two pieces. Shape the pompom.

EMBROIDERY
Embroidery is a simple way of making a garment look more personal. It is most common to add embroidery in a contrasting color, it can look very elegant with embroidery in the same color as the garment. You can use different kinds of stitches to create the patterns and shapes you want: Kitchener stitch, cross-stitch, French Knot, stem-stitch, or chain stitch, as pictured. The various stitches can also be combined into flowers and similar details.

Embroidery can also be used to strengthen edges or to hide flaws in a finished garment. The latter is practical when you do not discover the mistake before you are finished knitting.

Use a blunt sewing needle when you embroider on knits.

1

2

3

Seamless tips

When you are knitting small garments in a rough yarn it can be an advantage to not have too many seams to deal with.

The side seams may be avoided by casting on for the front and back piece at the same time, and removing 4 st for the seams, which you will not need. After this, you knit in one piece up until the first cast off for the armholes, which will now be 2 st under each arm. Continue by knitting the front and back piece separately following the instructions.

The shoulders can be knitted instead of sewn together. In that case you drop the cast off for the shoulder on the back piece, and place it to the side with a needle left in the work. When the front piece is ready you place the front shoulder straight against the top of the back shoulder, and hold the two needles next to each other in one hand. A third needle in the other hand is used to pick up 1 stitch from each piece and knit a garter stitch through both, repeat this, mask off by lifting the first knitted stitch over the other on the third needle, knit a new garter stitch through a st from both pieces. Cast off and so on. Make sure that you do this cast off quite tight, if not, the shoulder may lose its shape.

The arms can be knitted in the round on a circular needle, this way you will not have an arm seam. In that case cast on 2 st less than the basic pattern, since you won't need it for the seams. You keep track on the increases under the arm through allowing a thread to run through the work. The cast off under the arm should be 2 st, after which you knit the arm cap back and forth as instructed.

How to knit

Basic knot

This knot is the beginning of the most common Swedish cast on.

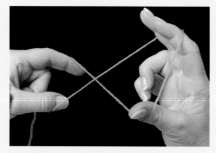

1. Hold the yarn so that it displays a loop.

2. Grip the yarn through the loop with your right hand.

3. Pull the yarn through and at the same time let the loop go from your right hand. You now have a basic knot.

4. Set the knot on the needle. Many use two needles to cast on more loosely.

Cast on

This cast on creates an even and minimally elastic edge.

1. Hold the yarn as pictured to start. The loose yarn is wound around your index finger and the yarn from the ball is wound around your thumb. Hold the yarn straight.

2. Thread the needle through the loop on the thumb.

3. Place the needle on top of the part of the yarn that you are holding with your index finger.

4. The yarn you are holding through your index finger should now be picked up with the needle and pulled through the loop by the thumb.

5. Release from the thumb and pull. You have now made one stitch. Take the yarn and wind it around your thumb once more to create the next stitch.

Knitted cast on

This cast on is what is referred to when the instructions say "cast on x stitches on the edge." Simply put, this is knitting a garter stitch in the stitch that already exists on the left needle.

1. Stick the right needle in the front stitch loop on the left needle.

2. Thread the right needle around the yarn that you are holding behind the left needle.

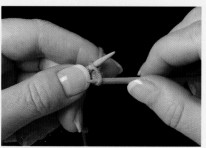

3. Pull the yarn through the stitch on the left needle so that a loop appears in front of the stitch.

4. Move the loop (which is the new stitch) from the right to the left needle. Repeat the procedure.

Garter stitch

1. From the front, thread the right needle though the first stitch, loop on the left needle.

2. Pick up the yarn that is laying over your left index finger with the right needle.

3. Pull the yarn through the stitch loop on the left needle. Let the stitch on the left needle slip, you now have the new stitch on the right needle.

Purl stitches

1. Hold the yarn in front of/above the left needle. From the back, thread the right needle in the first stitch loop on the left needle.

2. Pick up the yarn that you are holding over the left needle.

3. Pull the yarn through the stitch loop on the left side.

4. You now have a loop on the right needle. Release the yarn from the left needle.

Increasing in the same stitch

This is the easiest increase there is. It is used almost every time the increase happens next to a seam.

1. Knit the start of a garter stitch but do not lift the stitch loop off the left needle.

2. Now stick the right needle down through the backstitch loop on the left needle.

3. Pick the yarn up and pull it through.

4. Release the loop from the left needle and pull loosely.

Increasing between two stitches

This increase is also quite simple, and it shows even less than the increase in the same stitch. This increase is used almost every time the increase is happening at the middle of a knitted piece.

1. Lift the yarn between two stitches so that it creates a loop over the left needle.

2. Thread the right needle through the stitch loop behind the left needle (if you stick the needle through the front stitch loop a small hole will appear). Pick up the yarn you are holding around the index finger.

3. Pull the yarn through.

4. Release the yarn from the left needle and pull loosely.

Decreasing by knitting two stitches together from the front

This is an elegant and almost invisible decrease. The two stitches you knit together will tilt to the right. If you knit two stitches together by threading the needle through the backstitch loop the stitches will tilt to the left.

1. Knit like you would a regular garter stitch, but do it with two stitch loops.

2. Pull the yarn through.

3. Release the loops from the left needle.

4. The decrease is almost invisible (stitch number 3 on the right needle is the result).

Regular straight cast off

This cast off provides a pretty and straight edge, and it is quite hidden. Make sure that you do not knit too tightly.

1. Knit two garter stitches.

2. Lift the first knitted stitch (the one to the right) over the left.

3. Release the stitch you just lifted over. Knit another stitch and now lift the stitch on the right of the two knitted stitches over the left.

Mitten with wedge

Thumbs may be knitted in two ways, with or without a wedge. Here we illustrate how to knit with a wedge—the more complicated option.

1. Mark where the thumb will be.

2. Increase 1 stitch by increasing between two stitches. Do this by both thumb marks.

3. Knit back and forth, increase on every straight row until the given number of stitches reaches between the thumb marks. The wedge is now ready.

4. Place the stitches of the wedge on a thread and wait to knit the thumb until the rest of the mitt is ready. Knit the mitt together behind the thumb wedge.

5. The stitches behind the thumb wedge are now knitted together and are displaying the mitt's palm. Continue upwards until the mitten is ready. You complete the same way you do for socks (see p.122). Then divide the stitches of the wedge on double pointed needles and knit the thumb with these stitches.

Knitting heels

The easiest and prettiest heel is the one that is often called heel with patch. A sock with this heel fits nicely and is not particularly hard to knit. Here we illustrate a sock; on a stocking the shaft should naturally be given more length.

1. The stitches are set evenly between the double-pointed needles. The heel patch is knitted over the two back needles, normally needle 1 and needle 4. You don't have to be that particular about what needle you begin with; the heel will become the back of the sock regardless of which needle you use, however, it is important that you make sure that every needle has an equal number of stitches.

2. Knit stockinet back and forth over the two back needles for as long as the instructions dictate. It is easiest to do this with two needles; in that case, place a marker thread between the two middle stitches.

3. It is now time to decrease for the heel. Continue knitting back and forth as dictated by the instructions, but increase by knitting 2 garter stitches together and then sl1, k1, psso (it will say which decrease should be used on which side). The number of stitches should decrease by 2 every time you knit 1 row from the straight side. The decreases are commonly done 5–6 stitches away from the outer stitch.

4. Continue decreasing on every other row until the number of stitches corresponds with the instructions. Now the decreasing for the heel is finished.

5. Now it is time to pick up the sides of the heel patch and return to knitting with 4 needles. The sphere-like figure you see right above the marker thread is the decreases done on the left side. The right side will look the same. Pick up the instructed number of stitches all the way down to the next needle. In this picture we picked up 5 st and we had four st left on the needle after the decrease.

6. Garter knit over needle 2 and 3 (the front of the sock) and later pick up along the heel patch side to knit the whole sock together.

7. Continue in stockinet around the whole sock. Decrease (most often on every other row) at the end of needle 1 through knitting 2 garter stitches together.

8. On needle 4 you do a decrease as well, but here through a simple slip 1, knit 1, pass the slipped stitch over.

Completing the toe

Completing the toe is done in the outer edge of the sock, but within the last st on every needle. Place the sock with the heel facing downwards so that you are sure that you are decreasing correctly. On the right edge as seen from above you slip 1, knit 1 and pass the slipped stitch over, on the left edge as seen from above, you knit two garter stitches together. The goal here is to make the stitches tilt inwards on both sides.
Do exactly the same from the bottom, slip 1, knit 1, and pass the slipped stitch over on the right edge and knit two garter stitches together on the left edge.

A quick overview of crochet

Crocheted edges are fun to do and are very pretty. Here follows a few hand moves that are needed for the patterns in this book. All crochet work starts with a basic knot; this is then followed by a series of chain stitches which will be the cast-on row of the crochet work.

Chain stitch

The chain stitch is the crochet
version of the cast on.

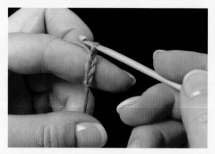

1. This is the starting point for
creating a chain stitch.

2. Grip the yarn end behind the
index finger with the crochet
needle. Pick the yarn up so that it
is twisted around the crochet
needle from the back.

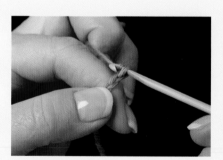

3. Pull through the stitch.

4. Do not pull too hard; it needs to
be easy to stick the crochet needle
in the stitch.

Single crochet stitch

These stitches don't build much height.

1. Starting point

2. Stick the crochet needle through the next stitch loop.

3. Pick the yarn up and pull it through the stitch loop on the crochet work. You now have 2 stitches on the crochet needle.

4. Take hold of the yarn once more and now pull it through both stitches on the crochet needle.

Double crochet stitch

The double crochet stitch is a way of increasing the volume of the crochet.

1. Place the yarn around the crochet needle from the back.

2. Stick the crochet needle through the next stitch loop; you now have 3 stitches on the crochet needle.

3. Get the yarn once more. Pull the yarn through 2 of the stitches on the crochet needle. You now have two stitches on the crochet needle.

4. Get the yarn again and pull it through the two remaining stitches.

5. The result.

This index describes the yarns we've used in the book.

In the descriptions under "materials," there are details of the yarn's gauge, thickness, and quality.
For more information about these yarns, contact the online distributors listed on the next page.

Yarn Index

Distributors

These websites will direct you to distributors around the world:
www.coatscrafts.com

www.knitters.org/resources/distributors
http://fiberarts.org/directories/suppliers/yarn.html?s=10
www.globalsources.com/suppliers/of-Fiber-Yarn/3000000179298.htm
www.ehow.com/how_6156448_buy-yarn-wholesale.html?ref=Track2&utm_source=ask

Knitting abbreviations

Cast off = cast off / bind off stitches
K = garter stitch
K2 tog = knit two garter stitches together
P = purl
P2 tog = knit two purl stitches together
YO = yarn over
St = stitch
Tog = together
Row = row/round
Sl1, k1, psso = slip 1 stitch, knit 1 stitch, pass the slipped
     stitch over, same as SKP

Crochet abbreviations

Ch = chain stitch
Dc = double crochet
Sc = single crochet
Sl st = slip stitch